To Rise above Principle

To Rise above Principle

The Memoirs of an Unreconstructed Dean

Josef Martin
(pseudonym)

University of Illinois Press
Urbana and Chicago

This book is printed on acid-free paper.

Library of Congress Cataloging-in-Publication Data

Martin, Josef.
    To rise above principle: the memoirs of an unreconstructed dean /
  Josef Martin
       p.   cm.
    ISBN 0-252-01507-X (alk. paper)
    1. Universities and colleges—United States—Administration.
2. Deans (in schools)—United States. 3. College administrators—
United States. I. Title
LB2341.M289 1988   87-27227
378.73—dc19   CIP

For the real J.M.,
a model of responsibility

Contents

Prologue

"The president has just had a phone-call from a parent," I heard the vice-president's voice saying over the phone.

Oh dear, I thought, and I bet the president believed everything he heard. And I bet you too tend to believe what you've just heard.

Perhaps it was my imagination, but I did usually sense that the V-P would take a student's word against that of a faculty member any day. It was really quite natural. The V-P still dealt fairly often with faculty; but not with the average professor, only with the hard cases and the inveterate complainers, and so he had acquired a jaundiced view of those who, at some distant time in the past, had been his colleagues and friends. It was also long in the past that he had taught students, and so he had forgotten the chicanery and ignorance and even impertinence of which some of them are capable. Ah, well. . . . It was all beside the point anyway, for this was the best and only V-P I had.

"The president called me," continued the V-P's voice, "but obviously you're the appropriate person to handle this. Maybe you should start by getting the parent's story yourself—and anyway, I think the president would appreciate your calling the parent so that he knows just how quickly we respond to these things. It's a Mr. Farwell, area code 753, telephone 902–6543.

His daughter Fiona is a drama major, and she's taking a course
from that peculiar fellow Albrecht—you might remember that
I wasn't sure at the time that we ought to tenure a man who
wears earrings. . . . Perhaps next time I'll trust my instincts
more. . . . Oh, well, water under the bridge. . . . Anyway, Fiona
Farwell is in this acting class and every student has to take a
certain number of parts during the semester, a range of parts;
and apparently they have to practice on modern stuff too, like
Hair and *Oh! Calcutta.* . . . Can you guess what's coming? Albrecht made every member of the class, Mr. Farwell's Fiona
included, do some acting in the nude. Entirely in the nude. And
the doors to the theater were locked so that no one could leave.
Farwell told the president that Fiona was quite hysterical when
she complained to him on the phone about it.

"Now, of course, I'm not going to prejudge what actually happened, you know I'm always careful not to do that, though the
story seems straightforward enough. These artsy people really
have no sense of responsibility, and sometimes I even wonder
if they know their own business. What's the point of acting in
the nude? Shakespeare didn't need tricks like that. . . ."

And the V-P continued thus for a while, trying to get rid of
some of his annoyance that life should present him with such
unforeseeable and unresolvable problems. I usually managed
to sympathize with him, once my initial anger over his prejudices wore off. His heart was truly in the right place, he worked
harder than most, and it wasn't entirely his fault that he hadn't
managed to transcend completely his early miseducation as an
engineer.

Should I talk to Albrecht's department chair immediately?
No, I decided, this was one of the rare occasions on which I
could leave a chair in blissful ignorance, even if for a very short
time only. Who knew, a miracle might eventuate so that the
chair need suffer no worry at all. So I called Mr. Farwell.

"Well, sir," I began, "I'm dean of the College of Arts and
Sciences here, and I've just heard about your call to the president. . . .

"Yes, of course, I understand. . . .

"Yes, I know, but we do have fairly well-established procedures that I must follow too. If there's any question of dismissing tenured faculty, we have to be very cautious about doing it right so that it won't get overturned. You know what the courts are like nowadays. . . .

"I can't tell you how often I long for the good old days myself. . . .

"But in any case, I would like to get all the facts at first hand, because I intend to handle this personally. . . .

"Well, let me just make some notes. Now, your daughter called you. . . .

"Oh. She didn't. You were just making your regular weekly call to her to find out how she was getting on. But she had just had this drama class. . . .

"Oh, you're not sure when it was. . . .

"No, no, of course it doesn't make any difference when. I hope you understand that I'm just trying to immerse myself in the situation. . . .

"Right. Tell me, and excuse my asking but I have daughters myself—and a wife, for that matter—is Fiona high-strung? Does she tend perhaps to sound hysterical on the phone? . . .

"Oh, she's particularly level-headed, takes after you and not after your wife. . . .

"And so she was talking really quite calmly until the matter of the drama class came up, and then she became quite evidently upset. . . .

"Oh, of course, of course, anyone would get upset at being forced to disrobe. I'm not questioning anything, just trying to get the full story. . . ."

And so on, until I had what seemed to be a reasonably full account, in the main as I had heard it from the V-P. Next, of course, I had to talk with Fiona. She proved to be in a state of considerable embarrassment when she came to see me at my invitation. Before I could get to the business at hand, she began to talk about it herself.

"I'm awfully ashamed that Daddy has done this. I asked him not to, but he said he was paying for this education and he just wasn't going to put up with it. I wish I'd never mentioned it to him; I keep forgetting how square he is. As soon as I said *Oh! Calcutta,* he asked if that wasn't the thing where some of the actors are nude; and then there was just no holding him back. I tried to tell him that it isn't at all the way people think, that everybody gets used to it very quickly, and that it's just another stage performance, but I don't think he was even listening to me anymore."

"Do you mean," I asked, allowing myself the first faint glimmerings of hope, "that you yourself were not too upset about it, or that you got over being upset?"

"Oh, I wasn't upset in the first place," Fiona responded, losing much of her initial embarrassment as she began to talk spiritedly and with enthusiasm. "I think it's marvelous that the faculty let us have experiences that are so much like professional theater. And Mr. Albrecht is really so good. Some of the people in class are a bit shy, and he said from the beginning that only volunteers would actually disrobe, and we also had the choice of wearing body-stockings if we wanted. . . ."

"Your father," I interrupted, "had the impression that everybody was required. . . ."

"Daddy just wouldn't stop fussing, and I don't think he listened properly. He was going on about taxpayers, and I thought he asked me whether it was a required course for my major, and I said of course it is. . . ."

"But didn't you tell him that the doors were locked, so that students who wanted to leave when they found out what was happening? . . ."

"Oh, gosh," came from Fiona, "no one wanted to leave. Anyway, we had known for weeks when this was going to be happening. We locked the doors so that no one outside of the class would come in by mistake."

Just one more thing to be quite certain about, I thought.

"Your father had the very distinct impression that you were very upset over the phone when you spoke to him about it; and that you hadn't been upset until you started to talk about this particular class or about this particular experience. He might even have used as strong an expression as 'hysterical'. . . ."

"Well," said Fiona, "of course I got upset when I heard his reaction and realized what I'd done by mentioning it to him. I mean, just immediately he was going to phone the president, and he hadn't even let me finish talking. And I certainly didn't want him to make any sort of fuss and embarrass me in front of the other students and Mr. Albrecht. . . ."

*   *   *   *   *

I rather enjoyed being able to assure the V-P that Albrecht was quite OK despite his earrings (and, though I didn't say it, despite the V-P's instincts). Then, however, I had to call on all the diplomacy I could muster as I not only filled in Albrecht's department chair on what had happened but also suggested to him that perhaps, just perhaps, this had been a lucky escape for all of us; that perhaps the experience of performing in the nude was not absolutely necessary, even nowadays, for every drama major—not, of course, that I would dream of trying to interfere with a department's control of its curriculum or an instructor's academic freedom in the classroom, but could they perhaps just informally talk the matter over in a faculty meeting, recognizing that the Philistines are still among us. . . .

Most difficult was my phone call back to Mr. Farwell. I began by playing my sometime role as a fellow arch-conservative, fighting a lonely and losing battle against the faddish forces of futuristic folderol, greatly concerned myself over the education my own daughters would receive, prayerful that sense would again and before long prevail in the modern world. I had to help him save face, of course, so I assured him that any parent, myself included, would have reacted and acted just as he did; that kids of college age don't know what's good for them and still need some protection. And then I told him how proud I was that our university had never succumbed to the fashion of mixed dor-

mitories, for example, which some other universities had be-
nightedly done. After a while I talked some about Fiona and
how favorable an impression she had made on me—mature, pol-
ite, so well brought up. . . . I think I talked long enough that he
was also not angry with her.

Would that it could always go so well.

*   *   *   *   *

I was reminded by this episode of a fellow dean whose College
of Arts and Sciences had been made smaller by the separation
from it of a College of the Dramatic, Fine, and Musical Arts.
Some of us had tried to sympathize with him about this setback
to the integrity of general and liberal education, not to mention
the blow to the dean's empire-building activities.

"Not at all," he assured us; "one of the best things that's ever
happened to me. I was all in favor of it. I've had to give up only
10 percent of my budget, but I'm now free of at least 50 percent
of the problems I used to have."

Introduction

Mr. Farwell's phone call to the president is the sort of thing that makes it interesting to be a dean. Amid much that is gratifying, amid much that is routine, amid much that is downright boring, there come these unexpected, indeed unforeseeable happenings—truths much stranger than fiction. Through being dean, I learned a lot—including some things I didn't particularly care to know and many things for which no one and no book had prepared me. A certain amount has been written about academe, about administration, even specifically about deaning; but nothing, so far as I know, has been written about these extraordinary incidents that flavor a dean's life. Hence this book.

I found it exhilarating to be dean. Having grown up intellectually omnivorous, I reveled in the opportunity to learn what it is that concerns scholars in the various disciplines. I was delighted to be able to converse with outstanding intellects in many fields—not only those on our faculty but also the distinguished visitors, among them winners of Pulitzers and Nobels and Wolfs.[1] I met enough Nobelists to sample the wide range of personalities among them: some who had remained entirely unspoiled by the prize; some who had come to take themselves rather too seriously; and at least one who had entirely succumbed to the temptation to assume guru-hood.

I found it exhilarating to be dean, to be in touch with a staggering bustle of activity. We hired faculty and department chairs, started new programs and revamped old ones, collared huge grants for curricular projects as well as for research. I was often conscious of being grateful for the opportunity to work with such competent people of ideals and integrity.

This book, however, is not a recounting of satisfactions and successes. For one thing, I wouldn't know how to make that even mildly interesting (except, perhaps, to those on the local scene). There is little disagreement over the virtues of strengthening liberal education, tightening and expanding the core curriculum, stimulating interdisciplinary activities, attracting people of quality, and so on; and my recounting of our many successes could only seem entirely banal and self-serving. Rather, I write of things that I learned through being dean, some of them things that I hadn't even known existed to be learned. I express views other than the common platitudes: sacred cows, I believe, should not be left to roam without hindrance; and even some modern and up-to-date emperors turn out also to be wearing no clothes rather than new ones.

I begin by relating some of the episodes I found surprising and therefore interesting; and I deliver myself of comments on them that I-the-dean could not always make at the time, be it as a matter of propriety or simply of kindness. Then—particularly in "Tribal Stereotypes"—I survey some of what I learned about differences among scholars in the several disciplines: I hadn't realized before just how various could be the approaches and values that characterize artists, say, or sociologists, by contrast with mathematicians, say, or chemists. In "Tricks of the Trade," I try to show that everyday matters can be approached with some consistency by holding consciously to a few very general principles—that academic and intellectual concerns should always be given clear primacy, for instance. And, finally, I try to suggest that, superficial appearances to the contrary, the compromises and imperfections widely attributed to administrators' machinations need not be entirely unprincipled.

I found it exhilarating to be a dean, and I hope that others can derive some pleasure or profit from reading about what I learned. The incidents recounted here are in their essentials true, but I have taken considerable liberties with the details of persons and places: I want to illustrate, not to gossip about particular individuals or institutions. That aim also mandates pseudonymous publication. Not all of the events I describe occurred at universities where I was employed, let alone during my tenure as dean; but I know that no such disclaimer will be accepted by everyone. There is also no other way than anonymity to protect the identities of some of the principal actors in the more singular episodes: although I've altered the personalities, the incidents themselves are a matter of record. Moreover, no matter that the personalities are partly or wholly my invention, I know that some people will erroneously think to find their characters accurately portrayed in these pages: the horoscopes in the daily newspapers and the "cold reading" practiced by palmists and psychics and stage mentalists prove that human behavior described in even the most widely applicable terms will be taken by many people to refer obviously and uniquely and specifically to themselves. When a former chancellor resorted, in a mystery novel, to such hoary stereotypes as "the meanest, cussingest coach" and the activist who takes up "any and every lost or unpopular cause," he was nevertheless accused of thereby portraying actual individuals: "We know who they are," said one of the college's officers.[2]

I prefer to avoid such hassles; I had to put up with enough similar ones on the job. *Honi soit qui mal y pense.*

Notes

1. Wolf Foundation prizes—in agriculture, chemistry, mathematics, medicine, and physics—are presented annually in Jerusalem for outstanding contributions on behalf of humanity. The selectivity and cash value approximate those of the Nobel prizes, but the Wolfs were

established much more recently—in the mid-1970s—and are not nearly so famous.

2. Scott Heller, "Author! Author! Shouts a College Town That Is Out for Ex-Chancellor's Blood," *Chronicle of Higher Education*, 26 November 1986, pp. 1, 15.

To Rise above Principle

1

Changing Careers

My interview for the deanship had gone well. I had prepared for it by getting quite clear about why I wanted the job and about how I would see the priorities and what things I would do personally and what I would delegate. There were few questions put to me that I had not thought about already, and only one that really surprised me: "You've been successful in research and in teaching, as a professor; why do you now want to change careers?"

It hadn't in fact occurred to me that becoming dean would be a change of career. I had always thought of academe as my career, as the environment in which I wanted to spend my life: a university's business is the work of the intellect, it seemed then and still seems obvious to me, and faculty and administrators share that work or career. Administrators ought to have been successful professors first, to learn what it's all about; then, for a time, they may devote themselves a bit more to the housekeeping chores before returning to the *real* work, that of thinking about substantive issues like the structure of matter or the nature of historical truth.

A comment I made years later to one of my old friends illustrates just how implicitly obvious all that is to me. We used to correspond by tape, and on one occasion I heard his voice saying in some amusement, "Do you know what you said on your last tape? That you were looking forward to the summer so that you could get some work done! Don't you think of your job as dean as involving work?"

"Work," of course, is a word that I'm not alone in using in some very different ways at different times. Administration is in one sense work, I admit, being enormously time-consuming and emotionally difficult. One's mind is never entirely free of concern over countless issues, many of them troublesome or potentially troublesome. Administration is "work" in the sense of being onerous and in the sense that one gets paid for doing it. But administration is not intellectually demanding, as scholarly work is demanding. In administration, the criteria are clear-cut and need no continual thought or reexamination: do what best serves the research and the teaching; handle any given situation on that basis and with the best information obtainable and with whatever amount of time happens to be available. This is in no way as difficult as striving to do or think what no one has done or thought before (and it is not nearly as important; my favorite aphorism here is, "Administration may be necessary, but it is certainly not important"). When I had spoken to my friend, I had used "work" in the sense of something that is intellectually challenging; after all, that's what the work of academe is supposed to be.

*   *   *   *   *

I've become increasingly confirmed in my bias that administrators should have been successful professors first. Of course, I've known a few—a rare few—exceptions, people who have a marvelous appreciation of and instinct for scholarship without having done much themselves. But even those few exceptions underscore the validity of the rule, for when those individuals made mistakes, I could usually understand why simply by recalling that they had never themselves actually done a scholar's job and therefore couldn't quite grasp some of its nuances.

Later I learned that the question about career change had indeed come from a man who had never himself been a full-fledged professor. But I also came to learn over the succeeding years the element of truth in the assumption behind his question: the administrator's time is spent so differently than the professor's that it cannot be obvious that both are serving essentially the same ends. And there are tricks to the trade of administration that need to be learned and for which time spent earlier as a professor is of no help; indeed, some habits acquired by a good professor are not appropriate to a good administrator.

I've come to appreciate, for instance, to what extent compromise is unavoidable. Not necessarily in the manner commonly talked of, however—that is, compromise with principle or integrity for the sake of expediency. No, the most inevitable compromises stem from dealing with professors who fall a little short of the ideal devoted professor who is not moved by self-interest, and with students who fall a little short of the ideal devoted student who wishes only to learn. Those professors and those students, however, are the only ones that deans have, and they must bend practice to that reality. Thus deans must usually defer to the ideal that the professors make the academic decisions, even when the professors and the resulting decisions are not ideal; deans must choose very carefully the few instances when they can allow themselves to act autocratically because the professoriate is too far from doing the ideal thing.

I've learned also that most of a dean's time is taken up with difficult people, in circumstances where no really satisfactory solution is in the cards.[1] I had much advice from friends when it was known that I was becoming a dean, even some advice that was quite good and not overly jocular; and I got a little benefit from reading in the scanty literature about deaning. But no one prepared me for the succession of intractable issues hinging on persons and personalities. Over a period of half-a-dozen years, I had a role in formally dismissing two tenured professors; in persuading another two to resign without formal hearings; in defending through countless hearings the denial of tenure to several clearly unqualified people; in responding to lawyers and to state and federal bureaucrats who were not civil and who were not right; in sharing the agonies of alcoholics and their families. I fired people I liked, people who had been loyal associates but who simply had to be replaced. And there were an uncountable number of only slightly less emotionally wearing instances. No one prepared me for that, and I suppose no one could have adequately done so. I would find myself thinking, Now I've seen everything; nothing can surprise me anymore, only to experience a novel surprise the next day or the next week.

If I were now to respond to that question asked at my interview—why I wanted to change my career—I would stick with my conviction that no such fundamental change is or should be involved; but I would take more cognizance of the things that deans find themselves doing. Administration, I would respond, is just the continuation of scholarship by other means.[2]

Notes

1. Quite early in my tenure, I had this excellent advice from my vice-president: don't judge the faculty or the students by those who come to see you. Mostly a dean sees the difficult or hopeless cases only; but the overwhelming majority of faculty and students are good and hard-working people who never cause any trouble.

2. Following Karl von Clausewitz: "Der Krieg ist nichts anderes als die Fortsetzung der Politik mit anderen Mitteln" (War is only the continuation of international politics by other means).

2

Learning

"I just came to welcome you to the university, and to introduce myself," he said.

How nice, I thought; but can that really be all? Perhaps it will turn out to be like the pleasant, handwritten letter my wife and I had received from an old resident of the town who hoped that we newcomers would like it as much as he had. I had been quite disappointed when my cynical wife had her suspicions confirmed: the old resident owned one of the local funeral parlors. He too was just welcoming us and introducing himself.

Clodon was an associate professor in his late thirties, though he looked even younger: hair cut unfashionably short, alert eyes, a smoothly unlined brow, well-spoken, charming even, with an unforced and ready smile. He told me how splendidly the university and his department had developed; how remarkably recent much of the important progress had been. He himself, though relatively young, was already one of the senior members of the department, had given of himself unstintingly, took pride in the developments, and was pleased that his contributions were appreciated by his colleagues.

I found myself beginning to relax, ready now to believe that Clodon really had come just to introduce himself—albeit as one of the most valuable members of the department whose promotion to full professor ought not to be long delayed. At least there seemed to be nothing that he wanted from me at the moment.

"Of course," he continued after a time, "not *everything* is completely fine and dandy. I'm beginning to get quite worried about our chairman; he seems to have changed lately. I was on the search committee that recommended him, and he was my top choice, and I've supported him since he took the job. Some of the others have started griping, and I've been defending him. But I have to admit there are some worrying signs." Among them: Clodon's last salary raise had been surprisingly small, and the chairman had given him a surprisingly heavy teaching load just because his rate of publication had been down a little recently.

"The research itself is going well, I'm excited about it, we're really into something new. But of course it will mean a year or two without anything actually getting into print. The chairman doesn't seem to understand that now is the time I need his support, before I've gotten far enough to get outside funding. I need some money, and I need some space, and I need a lighter teaching load to get this thing launched properly."

But (I was relieved to hear) Clodon didn't want me to do anything; he was just filling me in, giving me some background. Just possibly I might hear more about it, if the chairman remained unsupportive, but he didn't think so. He and the chairman were both reasonable people, they got on well, and he was sure it would all work out.

I did hope he was right about that, I told him, because that was really the only good resolution for these things. I expressed cautious sympathy, telling him of a few of the troubles I myself had had with department chairs when I had been a proper professor rather than an administrator.

After Clodon left, I looked at his personnel file. Most of those files were in slim folders: letter of appointment, vita, annual salary notifications, routine letters of thanks for serving on committees. Clodon's file, however, was massive. What he had told me was true enough: virtually a "founding father" of the department, much serving on important committees; also correct that his salary raises had gotten smaller over the years. But the other side of the story was told by records of innumerable complaints by Clodon to a succession of deans about a succession of Clodon's department chairs; of formal appeals for higher salary raises and lower teaching loads and different teaching assignments and more space and money for his research. I was struck by the rather sensible, even good-humored tone of most of his letters of complaint; just as in his conversation with me, so also had he assured my predecessors that there was not anything fundamentally wrong, that he and the chair were reasonable people, that they respected and understood one another, that the problems were simply specific little issues on which the chair was unaccountably mistaken, perhaps misled by some of Clodon's colleagues. If only the dean could make the chair see the error of his judgment on those little practical matters, everything would again be hunky-dory and the department would thrive. Certainly there was never any ill will on Clodon's part. He was well able to keep personal friendship for the chair secure, despite these particularities on which they didn't quite see eye-to-eye.

I could easily empathize with Clodon: I'd also been a good researcher and a good teacher and an eminently valuable and reasonable member of the faculty, yet I, too, was unfortunately saddled at times with department chairs whose judgments were not always sound, especially over my salary, money for travel, research support, and the like. But I was also reminded uncomfortably of Adrian, who had been a colleague, slightly senior to me, when I first attained a faculty position.

Adrian and I both did research in the same field as the chairman, and sometimes we published separately and sometimes jointly. About half the time, Adrian treated me as his closest friend and confidant: he talked to me of the chairman's faults, of his dubious support for higher salaries or promotions for us, of his decreasing mastery of research as his administrative burdens grew, of his inclination nevertheless to have his name put on "our" publications, of his neglect of the long-unchanged curriculum. The other half of the time, Adrian made clear that he saw through me: that I was trying to become the chairman's favorite, to displace Adrian who had been there longer, to freeze Adrian out of the communal research, to get my name first or solely on some of the publications. All that and more in tones of man-to-man, sensible understanding—he regarded me as a friend, indeed his closest friend, and understood my need to establish a career, and if that meant being unfair to him, well, that was the way of the world, he understood and didn't hold it against me and I wasn't to worry about it. We had important causes in common that transcended those little issues of personal competition. After all, we were among the rare few who really understood about quality, meaningful research, and rigorous teaching, and we would wage those good fights against the Philistines.

Our chairman had assured me that Adrian was paranoid, indeed paranoid schizophrenic; and he had shown me a description in some weighty tome of what that term meant.

Was Clodon more like me, I wondered now, or was he more like Adrian?

                    *   *   *   *   *

A few months after Clodon's visit, I had a call from his chairman.

"I'm awfully sorry to have to trouble you with something like this, but I don't know what to do about Clodon. We've just finished getting a little lab ready for Swenson, who joined us this fall, and now Clodon has moved some apparatus into that lab and he refuses to move it back out."

I hurried over to the department, and the chairman showed me the "lab" at issue—a cubicle about eight feet square with a small bench on which stood a few gadgets decorated with a sign: DON'T TOUCH UNDER PAIN OF DEATH.

I walked over to Clodon's office and knocked. Clodon opened the door and greeted me with every sign of genuine pleasure.

"Oh, how nice to see you over here. Are you having a look around the department?"

"Well, actually," I said, "I've come because of some fuss about space assigned to Swenson that you've apparently occupied."

Clodon expressed surprise. "You mean our chairman made you come over here just for that? Why didn't he just speak to me about it? It's really getting ridiculous how he avoids contact with me. We're surely reasonable, grown-up people who can negotiate issues with one another. I really don't know what's going to happen to the department if he keeps on this way, giving you the idea that we can't manage our own affairs."

"I'd been given to understand," I said matter-of-factly and poker-facedly, "that the chairman had spoken to you and that you had refused to move."

"Good heavens!" sighed Clodon. "See, that's just what I've been talking about. He just doesn't understand how to interact with people on a reasonable basis, how to negotiate differences of opinion. Whatever will he say or do next! Sure, we've talked about space problems, and he mentioned that Swenson will need someplace for her lab work when her apparatus gets here, and he asked me about that little cubicle, which apparently is all I can get for my own research. I told him that of course I'd need some substitute space in exchange, but that I was sensitive to the needs of new, young faculty and would certainly want to do what I could to help out, and that we should talk about it again when Swenson had her equipment ready to set up, but that I saw no reason to move before then just to have the space sitting empty. . . . Why on earth would the chairman want to get you involved in such a simple and routine bit of departmental business?"

"Well," I said, "I'm quite relieved that there really is no problem, that you're determined to be cooperative. May I tell him that you're quite prepared to let Swenson take over that space, and that you'll move your equipment within the next day or so?"

"Why, of course," responded Clodon lightly. "There was never any question about it; just about the timing. I didn't see why it was necessary to move work in progress before Swenson had her equipment quite ready to go. But since our chairman had you make this unnecessary trip over here, I want you to be completely reassured. In fact, I'll move my stuff out tonight."

I thanked Clodon and went to report my success to the chairman. The latter seemed surprised.

"I don't understand it. Why would he move when you ask him but not when I did?"

*   *   *   *   *

Time passed and Clodon's personnel file continued to expand. His research was always going well, but it didn't get published; he was never quite ready to seek grants from funding sources outside the university; occasionally his teaching met with less than high acclaim from the students; and his pay raises were approaching zero. Then things turned more serious. Clodon put in writing what was essentially an ultimatum: his career would be seriously jeopardized if his research continued to be hampered by the chairman's lack of support and his assigning Clodon such a heavy teaching load, and this letter was to serve notice that Clodon simply would not accept, beginning next term, teaching assignments amounting to more than two courses per semester.

I talked with him; perhaps I even pleaded with him. I told him that refusal of teaching assignments could be grounds for dismissal, tenure or no tenure. I counseled him to use all available channels of appeal: if disinterested parties supported Clodon, he would get relief; if not, he ought to accept the teaching load as part of the environment, not as mistaken judgment by the chairman.

Then one semester, after further written protest of his teaching schedule, Clodon simply did not show up for one of the classes assigned to him. There were meetings, indeed many meetings: Clodon, the chairman, me, the vice-president, the university's attorney, Clodon's lawyer, the local AAUP officers, the faculty ombudsman, various of Clodon's colleagues, in all sorts of combinations; hundreds of person-hours, quite literally, were spent on meetings.

Clodon remained adamant. Seeing no alternative, we went for dismissal for cause and set in motion the further lengthy prescribed procedures: formal written charges, with replies and clarifications; an informal hearing by a faculty committee, to advise whether dismissal proceedings should continue. "Yes," they said, so a letter of dismissal was sent. Clodon asked for the formal hearing to which he was now entitled, and a hearing committee was selected through mutual agreements and challenges.

I was far from sure how it would turn out. The chairman was nervous, the vice-president was vaguely and unconvincingly reassuring, the university's attorney was as opaquely legalistic as ever. The chairman could sometimes make a bad impression if he got rattled, as well he—or anyone, for that matter—might in a formal hearing under cross-examination by an experienced attorney. The documentation, I thought, could not convey just how impossibly disruptive Clodon had become to the department. And faculty serving on such hearing committees have a way of automatically taking the side of the professor—any professor—against the by definition wicked administration. What might Clodon's lawyer make of the higher teaching loads assigned to Clodon in comparison with most of his colleagues? Could such academically desirable approaches as individually assigned work-loads survive legalistic notions of equity?

Indeed, as the hearings began, I was not reassured by the attitude of the hearing panel, by the questions they asked, by the naive but innuendo-laden sallies from Clodon's lawyer. Finally the university's case was presented, and then it was time for the defense to make its case, and Clodon's lawyer called on him to give a brief summary of the situation as he saw it.

Clodon began to speak in his usual fluent, sensible, good-humored, understanding manner. He regretted that it had come to this, that the time of so many people had to be wasted; but he was also glad that at last a proper settlement would be reached once and for all—although he was sorry that the chairman would be embarrassed, because Clodon had nothing against him personally and understood the problems he had in the department. Indeed, one of Clodon's sorrows was that the chairman had not allowed him to contribute to the department in the fullest possible way. He would gladly shoulder heavy committee duties, as he had in the old days when he and a few others had built the foundations for this very good department, but he simply couldn't do it with such a heavy teaching load. He had always been a popular teacher, and it was the chairman's fault that Clodon's enrollments and student evaluations had begun to decline; no one could do a really first-rate job in the classroom with such a heavy load. And it was not selfishness on Clodon's part to want support and time for his research: the department and the university would benefit from the publication of his work, which was right at the forefront and had the potential to be really productive once it found the needed support. It was a pity that the chairman, who had started out so well, seemed to have lost his earlier appreciation of Clodon's contributions, had listened to the wrong people, and had mounted a campaign to hinder Clodon's work and to hamper his career. The chairman thought that he was being subtle, but Clodon had seen through him from the beginning. Even when he had been appointed, Clodon had realized that the chairman was not fully conversant with up-to-the-minute research or with what the students should be taught, but he had thought that with his help and advice the department and the chairman could nevertheless thrive. Unfortunately the chairman had made the wrong people his confidants, and Clodon's advice was taken as criticism, and so Clodon had dropped out of committee work to concentrate on his research. He hadn't been bitter or offended, of course; he understood the situation and was just going to contribute in other ways until his judgment on departmental matters was again called on and recognized as valid. But the chairman had begun a campaign of persecution. Research funds that Clodon needed were instead given to newly appointed faculty—who, of course, needed help to get started, Clodon was all for that, but not at the expense of the important ground-breaking effort he had mounted, which needed departmental support until the first results could be published and grants would come in. And the chairman had assigned to others the space Clodon needed, using the excuse that Clodon had no graduate students, although Clodon knew about the machinations that had led to that: the chairman and the other faculty had advised students not to work with Clodon; they had insinuated that Clodon had no grants and didn't get publications for his students. But none of that was his fault. He had an excellent program at the forefront of research, but not even the most excellent program could get anywhere without space and students and money. Clodon had spent some of his own money on needed equipment, but he couldn't keep on doing that—not that he minded, he was in academe because he wanted to teach and to do research, he didn't care about money, otherwise he would be out in industry making much more. He had complained about his salary not because of the money but because it was symbolic of the chairman's lack of appreciation for his contributions—even though he had been the chairman's strongest supporter when he was first appointed and had consistently defended him against the other faculty. But the chairman had turned against him, and Clodon now had no option but to expose his machinations. Not only had he taken away his research funds and his space for research, not only had he given him an impossibly heavy teaching load, not only had he discouraged graduate students from working with him, but the chairman had tried to make things personally unpleasant for Clodon. He had made him teach courses that he wasn't really qualified to teach, though of course he could teach them, and do a good job, because he was not only a popular teacher but one who set high standards and gave students the very latest information and understanding. Yet the chairman had assigned to others those upper-level and graduate and special-topic courses and had made his teaching schedule as unpleasant as possible, with classes almost every day of the week and scattered throughout the day, instead of clustered (as they were for the other faculty) to allow reasonably connected periods of time for research. Even then, the chairman kept harassing Clodon. When he knew Clodon was in his office, the chairman would dial the number of the telephone in the next room, even though he knew there was no one in that room, and let the phone ring and ring and ring, just so Clodon couldn't have any quiet time to plan his research or to prepare his lectures. And when Clodon began to spend more time at home, to get away from the harassment and to do his work uninterrupted, the chairman would comment about Clodon's lack of interest in the department, and he would even telephone him at home. Of course, when Clodon would pick up the phone there would be nobody on the line, but Clodon knew it had been the chairman wanting to disturb him even at home. But he wasn't going to get away with it any longer. Clodon was glad that at last he could have his say, even though it meant exposing the chairman, against whom he had no personal animosity. . . .

After a while, I almost stopped listening. Glancing around the room, I saw various mixtures of surprise and embarrassment on the other faces. Clodon's lawyer was poker-faced; perhaps he had practice at that, if he gave other clients as poor advice as he had evidently given Clodon, since he had evidently been unable to grasp what was going on when Clodon briefed him. I recalled the court-martial scene in *The Caine Mutiny,* particularly the filmed version in which Bogart gave such a splendidly insightful and sympathetic rendering of the unfortunate, paranoid Queeg; as I later discovered, no fewer than three of the other people present in the hearing room independently made that same comparison. I found myself also reminded by Clodon's youthful appearance, to which his unlined brow contributed, of a contention once put to me by a corrections officer: that adults who bear no worry-lines on their foreheads tend to be criminals, idiots, psychopaths, or the like. "They never worry because, to themselves, they are never at fault about anything and they never feel guilt."

Eventually the presiding officer called for adjournment. The panel found against Clodon, and he left the university. Those of us who had been closely involved in the affair kept rehashing it for some time, troubled that no one had recognized much sooner the now-evident paranoia, wondering whether anything could have been done to help Clodon and to prevent his professional demise. But we usually concluded that nothing could have been done. Any notion that professional psychological counseling, for example, might have helped always foundered in recognition of the fact that Clodon and his departmental colleagues themselves had their professional expertise in psychology.

*   *   *   *   *

A few years later, my in-basket brought me a reminder of Clodon. He was a candidate for employment as a personnel consultant with a large company, and the form letter asked me (1) to confirm that Clodon had been in our employ; (2) whether his services had been satisfactory; (3) whether we would again hire him.

As I recall, I spent quite a long time over my response.

3

A Few Dollars More

Associate Professor Shabda was quite visibly upset. "Professor Jones, he has behaved so much unprofessionally, I ask that you do something."

For several years now, Shabda had wanted to be promoted to full professor. But it had proved difficult to get unequivocally enthusiastic evaluations of his published research, and his department remained divided on the issue of recommending him for the promotion.

"I talk to all the full profs," he told me now, "and some say they will vote my way, but others say they would have but not with the letters so far from outside. I find out, it is almost even split, and only Prof Jones tell me he not sure yet. So I explain to him how important is this to me, my work is good, plenty of publication, I am too old to be associate still, I would do whatever I have to get promoted, I have really done whatever needed. So Prof Jones ask, how much in money a promotion worth? And I tell him, I have no interest in money, I want only the fair title I deserve, if I get promote I don't care about increment, he can have it. So he say, sound to him like good deal, in that case he certainly vote my way. . . .

"So I get very angry now when I hear department has voted, I not get recommendation, and so I know Prof Jones he breaks his word to me and vote other way. Deal should be deal."

Long ago, one of my friends had assured me that administrators could survive by holding their hands almost as though praying, tips of the fingers together, periodically nodding the chin toward the hands, and never saying anything except "I see," "Go on," "Hmmmm," and the like. I had adopted that stance soon after Shabda had started talking, and I continued to temporize when he had stopped.

"Of course, you realize, much as I sympathize with your disappointment and understand the seriousness and urgency from your point of view, even just for the sake of proper procedure I must go slowly and carefully here. And I must try to foresee what approach will work best, because you understand that some people might say that you yourself ought perhaps not to have entered into such an arrangement. I take it that I am free, from your point of view, to talk about this with Professor Jones?"

I certainly was, Shabda assured me. But that assurance didn't really help me: how on earth could I broach the matter with Jones? I thought I knew him rather well, and this sounded completely out of character, in fact, quite incredible. I certainly didn't want him to think for even a moment that I would give any credence to such a tale about him. So I concluded that I had better not be straightforward with Jones but rather hope that an oblique approach would get me somewhere.

I arranged to run into Jones quite by chance, and we exchanged the usual small talk.

"I hear," I said after a while, "that your department is as unanimous as usual about its recommendations for promotion."

He grimaced. "Actually, this time there's good reason for our being so divided. It's not internal politics—don't smile, I'm really serious—but we keep getting mixed reviews of Shabda's publications. If only he wouldn't publish all those quickies;

some of his articles are apparently quite good. But you know
how he is, if someone tells him that, he interprets it as trying
to hold him back. He really is awfully anxious about losing
face, being an associate so long. He was talking to me about
that just a few weeks back, and that it wasn't a matter of the
money, he apparently has plenty of that, in fact he said he
would gladly do without a raise if that would help get him
promoted. I tried to get him to be a bit less desperate about it;
I tried to joke about it a bit, told him I didn't really think the
vice-president would go for that, not that I would place all that
much stock in the V-P's integrity, but just that it wouldn't
make enough difference to the university's payroll. Well, at
least he seemed to smile at that, so I continued about how he
was really pretty lucky not to need the money, not everyone
in the department could say that, some people seemed to be
having such a rough time with inflation that maybe he could
even buy a few votes with that promotion increment, if tuition
costs kept going up I might even have to accept such an offer
myself, what with two kids in college now and another two to
go in a few years' time.

"Anyway, I thought I'd made him feel a bit better just by
listening some and joshing with him. He seemed to relax a bit
and smiled and thanked me for understanding his situation.
But the way he's taken the decision now, I'm afraid anything I
did was purely temporary. He seems just as frantic about it
now as he ever has been."

Ah-ha, I thought, Rashomon again;[1] never, never, never
imagine that you have any facts until you've heard at least two
different versions.

"You know," I felt it safe to venture, "perhaps he didn't
realize you were joking. There are places where cash for votes
isn't regarded as totally dishonorable, if I haven't forgotten all
of what I once knew about politics; it seems to me that even in
this country, Chicago, say. . . ."

"Oh, no," Jones brushed it aside. "Shabda's been here long
enough to know we don't do things that way. He's really quite

acculturated, and I told you I think he's even developing a sense of humor.''

And, I thought, only God knows how, it's now my job to acculturate him further and hasten the development of his sense of humor.

* * * * *

I shared this story with one of my wisest and most discreet colleagues, telling it as though about another institution.

"Don't be so goddamned smug and self-righteous," he surprised me by saying. "You're just as culturally parochial as the next guy. You have this prejudice against societies that have worked out a satisfactory mode of functioning through such mechanisms as paying cash for individual value received, a mechanism you denigrate by calling it 'bribery.' Does our own society function all that well without bribery? How do you think you would get on, trying to explain to Shabda why the payroll office doesn't do the payroll right; why the dean of admissions does the opposite of what we want; why the accounting department is always two months behind? Do you think he could understand why you, in your exalted position, turn purple in the face thrice a week just because some petty bureaucrat has been both petty and bureaucratic? Don't you in fact agree that it would be better if we had Shabda's system here? Wouldn't you really like it if you could get accounting and admissions and the computing center and payroll and personnel and all the others to do their jobs properly, just by slipping them a few dollars more?''

Note

1. *Rashomon*, a film directed by Akira Kurosawa, won the Grand Prize at the Venice Film Festival in 1951. In the film, the same event is recounted by each of four participants, and clearly each version is true for the one who tells it; yet the four stories differ drastically from one another. This is an essential lesson for a dean to learn, and quickly. Never assume that you are hearing the truth just because the speaker is entirely sincere. What that person believes to be true

rarely or never is; at best it is one aspect of what really happened, but it is never the whole truth, nor even those parts of the truth that are essential for the dean to know. Moreover, the truly pathological liars (of whom there are fortunately very few) convey an unparalleled impression of total sincerity. At the same time, no story should be dismissed out of hand just because it seems too bizarre. Superficially unbelievable events can prove to be explicable in entirely mundane ways if one knows something of human nature—as marvelously illustrated, for example, by G. K. Chesterton's tales of Father Brown.

4

Responsibility

The semester was nearly over, the weather was reliably decent, and I was beginning to unwind, to look forward to the summer, and to having some time to call my own. The scheduling of my time by others I found to be one of the most wearing and wearisome aspects of deaning. It's often said that administrators shouldn't just react to problems, that they should look ahead and plan strategically and set the grand schemes in motion. But those same administrators are also expected to be endlessly available: to faculty at all times, to students as necessary, to honor societies and the AAUP and all the other organizations, to give a welcoming address to any sort of conference or group. Most of the time, despite the marvelously protective care and excellent judgment of my secretary, my days were booked solid. It was rare that I could enjoy a nonbusiness lunch,[1] or get my in-tray cleared during office hours; nor could I always call the evenings my own; nor, by any means, the weekends. Having almost no control over my time was another side of deaning for which no one and nothing had prepared me.

I'm truly not suggesting that administrators work harder than busy faculty, nor even that they work longer hours. In fact, I spent at least as much time, when I was a faculty member, on all the things connected with teaching and research and com-

mittee work and professional organizations. But as a professor
I could schedule almost all of my time just as I wished, deciding
for myself what to do when. Not much more than a dozen hours
of the average week were arranged for me by others—lectures
and a few meetings; for the rest, I was in control. Sometimes I
chose to work until the small hours of the morning, especially
if my lectures were in the afternoons and I could sleep late; or
I could work on weekends and in exchange go fishing on one
of the weekdays when I had no classes. But as dean, five days
a week of my time, from 8 A.M. to 5 P.M., belonged entirely to
others, and many bits of evenings and weekends too.

I found, moreover, that the myriads of things in process were
always close to the surface of my mind and would break through
while I was reading a book, or trying to write an article, or at
any other time. That is another facet of the difference: as a professor, I had many fewer different kinds of things on my mind.
Ideas about my research or about my classes would also come
to me at any time of day or night, but not much else; my mind
was occupied with only a few things, and largely with mutually
related ones, whereas a dean's mind is always full of many not-
so-closely-related matters. Thus, many of the thoughts that came
unbidden to me as dean were annoyingly distracting even when
they were ultimately useful.

*   *   *   *   *

At any rate, here I was unwinding as the end of the academic
year approached, enjoying a Saturday morning at home in the
knowledge that I would have caught up with things in a few
weeks and might even be able to get some of my "own" work
done. Then I was called to the phone.

"Sorry to call you at home," I heard Jack Fraser, chairman
of one of our larger departments, say. "I hate to disturb you,
but I thought you needed to know: Duffy has just faked his student evaluations."

In my lighthearted, end-of-the-year mood, my first impulse
was to laugh with relief. Calls at home, beginning with "I thought
you needed to know"—or, more bizarrely, "I thought you would

want to know"—had sometimes meant the unexpected death of some valued person, or a professor arrested on a morals charge, or an assault perpetrated by a faculty member on a student—or vice versa—or a professor needing to be hospitalized, or the like. So a mere faking of student evaluations was almost welcome. Perhaps we could just give Duffy a spanking and send him home to bed?

But then my mind started to work again, and I asked for details, and especially for proof. Was Fraser sure? How had he found out? Had he confronted Duffy?

Alas, it was all true. When I spoke later with Duffy, he admitted it; the only excuse he could offer was that it had been a momentary aberration. He asked for clemency. "Don't cut me off from the profession," he pleaded. "I've never done anything like this before, and I never will again, I promise most sincerely. If you fire me, I won't be able to get another job in my field." And, looking me straight in the eye, he continued very seriously, "My profession is my life; my life is in your hands."

You bastard, I thought, you're trying to shift responsibility onto me. You do the cheating, but you want me to be responsible for the consequences. And, callously now, I thought further that the university and the profession would be well rid of him. Duffy had never been one of my favorite people. Judged quite good at one time, he had succumbed to the madness of the late 1960s and early 1970s, seeking to get the attention and approval of the students by growing his hair long, dressing sloppily, wearing the latest slogans on both lapels, and emoting instead of thinking. He had given up scholarship in favor of academic and secular politics and had become a genuine nuisance in his department, always ready with petitions to and criticisms of one chair after another.

You bastard, I thought, you're going to cause me sleepless nights wondering whether I want to fire you because I disapprove of you generally or because it really is the right response to what you've done. And the implication that you've thought about suicide isn't going to help me much.

*   *   *   *   *

The chief point at issue, it seemed to Fraser and to me and to the vice-president, was that none of us could ever trust Duffy again about anything; his promise now of good behavior in the future simply carried no conviction at all. Nor could we avoid suspicions about what he might have been dishonest about in the past, without having been found out. Perhaps he had often faked evaluations? How much integrity had he brought to bear when grading papers?

Fraud in research or plagiarism in scholarship are acknowledged reasons for dismissing faculty, but was faking evaluations somehow less serious? The same issue of trust was surely central to all those matters. Do we really believe that teaching is as important as scholarship? If so, how important is the integrity of our means of assessing it? What would we do to a student who cheated on an examination? Under the honor code, in point of fact, that student would be dismissed from the university and would find it quite difficult to gain admission to another decent college. Was Duffy's cheating somehow less serious, or were the pressures on him somehow greater? And if Duffy was ready to forge better student evaluations, could we trust him not to seek such better evaluations through, for example, easy grading?

In the end, we concluded that Duffy ought to go, because we could not rely on him to be honest about anything. Honesty is absolutely necessary in scholarship and in teaching, and the presumption of honesty must pervade academe. Duffy had enough sense to take the opportunity we gave him to resign, and I found myself profoundly grateful to him that he didn't put us through all the fuss of hearings and lawyers and the rest.

*   *   *   *   *

Already before this episode, I had thought much about the degree of my personal responsibility for my various actions as dean. I could usually empathize with those people who were denied tenure, for example, understanding the blow to self-respect and the well-founded anxieties about whether another teaching job could be found; and I always shuddered at such strain placed on a young person, usually with a young family to support, almost inevitably still in debt, perhaps being forced to look for an entirely different way of earning a living. How could I, by denying tenure, place a human being in such a situation?

I'm not sure, in point of fact, that I ever could. But the question is entirely hypothetical as well as rhetorical. I, the person with the emotions, was not called upon to say "Tenure" or "No tenure"; it was the dean who was charged with assessing the credentials of the candidates and judging whether those credentials matched the fairly well defined expectations long ago made quite plain and public knowledge by the university. Now I happened to be the dean, but that gave me no warrant to reach decisions based on my human emotions rather than on what it said in my job description.

If tenure had to be denied, moreover, then the responsibility lay with the candidate, not with those who formally assessed his achievements and certainly not with me personally. The university's criteria were clear enough, much the same as in most good universities: publish or perish but do a good job at teaching too. If, for example, a person had decided to make money during the summer months instead of writing for publication, or if a person just wasn't good enough, well I could hardly take the blame or the responsibility for that. Nevertheless, some of the unsuccessful candidates for tenure would come to tell me what "I was doing to them"; and I had to be perpetually on guard not to feel as though that was actually a proper description of the circumstances.

So when Duffy told me that I held his life in my hands, he hadn't quite hooked me. I already knew, from analogous situations, that the responsibility was his, not mine; I only had the job of deciding what the academy's proper response was. Admittedly, it did occur to me that this might be the occasion when one of my nightmares came true: a suicide at least peripherally induced by something I-the-dean had or had not done. But I had been rather clear from the outset that any responsibility for the situation rested pretty squarely on Duffy. He had not been mentally or emotionally or physically ill, nor had he claimed to be. The manner of the fraud clearly indicated premeditation— we have safeguards that prevent professors from having access to those evaluations before the final grades have been awarded, and it had called for some clever preparation to vitiate those safeguards. Duffy had been in command of himself and thus had to bear the full responsibility for being asked to resign.

*   *   *   *   *

Of course, I'm not proposing that administrators harden their hearts and shut off their emotions; but I am suggesting that they differentiate clearly between grounds for their official recommendations or actions and grounds for feeling empathy with another human being. I-the-dean bore the responsibility for taking the most disinterested view possible, but not for what might happen to an individual if that view led to the loss of a job— always recalling, too, that recommendations on such serious matters had to run the gauntlet of at least another couple of people or committees. Not feeling personally responsible for these misfortunes of others, I believe, also helped me to empathize with them more freely in human terms. I would listen to the disappointed candidates for as long as they wished and express sympathy and try to find useful suggestions to make. I could hardly have managed that if I had felt all the time that I had freely and on subjective grounds chosen to deny these people their jobs.

Note

1. I found that there is, after all, such a thing as a free lunch, but it is bad for one's health, in one way or another. There are also free breakfasts for deans, invariably at an hour when civilized people are still in bed.

5

Signs and Styles

I once served under a dean—let's call him Peter Tripper—
who was, I thought, rather a poor dean. He avoided personal
contact with the faculty as much as he could and was obviously
uncomfortable whenever he couldn't. By the department chairs
he was regarded as the administration's errand boy, bringing
down instructions but never taking their views back upstairs.
In person he was a most forgettable man. But what I have not
forgotten, what struck me as curious when I first became aware
of his existence, is that the memoranda he sent to the whole
faculty were always signed "Pete T." That mode of signing struck
me as incongruous: Tripper had never met me, yet here he was
putting himself on a first-name basis with me. Since then, I have
come to see how that signature revealed some significant things
about Peter Tripper's view of himself and of his role as dean.

* * * * *

Dean Peter Tripper had the choice of signing his memoranda
in a number of different ways:

1. "Peter Tripper" or "P. Tripper"
2. "Peter T." or "Pete T."
3. "Peter" or "Pete"
4. "PT"
5. "P" or "T"

Some of those modes are quite impersonal; others have a more personal flavor. How to choose among them? And does it matter?

It does matter, because the signature symbolizes the nature of the relationship between the sender and the recipient of the communication, just as does the use of names in conversation. For example, professors do not usually expect their students to address them on a first-name basis: one expects to hear, "Professor Tripper, I'd like you to change my grade," not "Pete, I'd like you to change my grade." Use of the first name implies a symmetry in the relationship, an equality of status and role, that use of the formal style of address does not.

When I first began to teach and to direct graduate students, I discussed that issue with a friend who was also beginning his academic career. He had made a point of asking his graduate students to address him by his first name; I thought that to be a mistake. And I was proven right when soon enough one of his students misinterpreted my friend's attempt to create a friendly and informal environment and began to tell him how he should plan his research, divide projects among the students, give credit for the students' work, and much else.

When I was dean, my assistant and associate deans and I were of course on a first-name basis; but in referring to them, I always used the formal mode—I would ask my secretary to phone "Dean Truly," not "Wanda." My secretaries always called me "Dean Martin," appropriately enough; and I could see them bristle when one particular assistant to the dean would address me in their presence as "Joe"—that assistant was not a member of the academic faculty and had no warrant thus to presume a more intimate status with me than that of the secretaries. Another assistant to the dean, however, understood perfectly: in the outer office or in the presence of others, she would address me as "Dean Martin"; when we were alone she called me "Joe," for we happened to have a social relationship as friends that anteceded and was independent of our relationship at work.

People in an institution should interact on the basis of what their jobs or tasks are, not on the basis of what their personal relationships happen to be: thus I should treat my secretary as a secretary, and she should treat me as a dean; our views about politics, religion, or the like are quite irrelevant, as it is also irrelevant whether we find one another attractive or interesting or good conversationalists. I should judge candidates for promotion only on the basis of their professional achievements; I should judge teachers on the basis of their effectiveness, not by whether I personally happen to like their styles or their jokes.

In a university, as in most institutions, everybody is not the same; in particular, some people have more authority than others. A mode of address that recognizes the asymmetry of authority need not be offensive; but a mode of address that is inconsistent with that asymmetry spells trouble, sooner or later, in one way or another. When a dean signs his memoranda "Peter Tripper" or "P. Tripper" or "PT," no one is moved to ponder the significance of it; no one pays any attention to the mode of signing, because it is appropriately impersonal, as official communications ought to be. These memos, after all, come from the Office of the Dean, not from whomever happens to be its current occupant. Such memos expound policy, or prescribe procedures, or explain official actions, or foreshadow institutional plans; they are not vehicles for the dean to communicate as a human being with other human beings about the weather or politics or religion or some private hobbyhorse. Memos are not occasions for the occupant of the dean's office to broadcast personal opinions; when memoranda convey opinion, it ought to be the opinion of the Office of the Dean, formed through the impartial interpretation of institutional goals and policies and criteria and procedures.

Among the impersonal forms of signing, "PT" rather than the longer modes is an appropriate recognition of how very busy a dean is.[1] But why stop there? Why not just "P" or "T"?

My experience of those who choose to sign with but a single initial leads me to conclude that this signifies a more aggressive and yet vulnerable ego than most of us would care to reveal even if we happen to be saddled with it. "PT," after all, is likely to apply to few if any other people in the college; "P" or "T" alone, however, could conceivably apply to dozens of others. Does Peter Tripper really want thus to emphasize that he is the only "P" or "T" who really matters? Or does he seriously expect us to believe that he is so busy that the omission of a single letter in the signature saves a useful amount of time? Still, any of these impersonal modes of signing can serve a dean's purpose; not so the use of such personal modes as "Peter" or "Pete" or "Peter T." or "Pete T."

Graphologists, semioticians, or psychologists will not need me to tell them what the use of such personal signatures on memoranda reveals about Peter Tripper:[2] that he thinks of himself as "just the same" as the faculty, or that he would like the faculty to think of him as "just one of them." In other words, he is uncomfortable about assuming and exercising the authority that goes with the Office of the Dean; or he has a strident need to be liked by his faculty; or, of course, both. He is evidently an other-directed person[3] and therefore has scant convictions about anything—for example, what a university ought ideally to be. He will act as he thinks the consensus is, not as the consensus ought ideally to be. Hence he will not be effective in creating consensus, and he will always be reacting rather than leading.

Or, at best, he will discover—as did my friend with his graduate students—that he made a mistake in trying to project informality: he will find himself being taken advantage of by witting or unwitting members of the faculty. For instance, if your department chair is an impersonal "CN" but your dean is "Pete," is it not more promising to take your complaints directly to Pete rather than to CN? And when you are talking to Pete, is it not difficult to keep in mind that he should not be free to deal directly with you in business matters but should respect the chair's role of authority in relation to you?[4]

If Pete wants to remain "one of the boys," then he has no business becoming dean. If he becomes dean, then he is no longer one of the boys; and if he tries to avoid that conclusion, then he will be dean in title only.

*   *   *   *   *

Just as the style of name usage has implications that not every administrator understands, so too are there features of the common language that bureaucrats typically overlook; for example, that enumeration of particulars inevitably implies something about items left off the list.

Our affirmative action people evolved a statement to be incorporated into catalogs, bulletins, brochures, and the like: "The university does not discriminate against employees, students, or applicants on the basis of race, sex, handicap, age, veteran status, national origin, religion, or political affiliation." Quite in vain did I point out the clear implication that we felt free to discriminate against, say, alumni, or perhaps relatives of students. And that we even felt free to discriminate against employees, students, or applicants, provided we did so on grounds other than the eight qualities specified in the statement.

We were also exhorted to make nondiscrimination and affirmative action explicit in all advertisements of positions. I evolved something that tried to make the point without resort to the usual hackneyed phrases: "Our aim is to attract the best candidates, without preconceptions as to race, national origin, or other irrelevant attributes; high qualifications for this particular position will be the sole criterion." But that advertisement did not pass muster with the affirmative action officers, who insisted that our ads state at the bottom, "An AA/EEO Employer."[5]

I asked, "Don't you think my words convey the same message? And more convincingly, because it's clear that we've thought about it instead of merely including a phrase that has come to be just another punctuation mark?"

"No"; and "no."

"Well, then," I ventured, "how about a slogan that conveys the same message but is less hackneyed? How about 'Here we practice virtue'?"

They thought I was joking.

*   *   *   *   *

TO: Dean Josef Martin
FROM: Vice-President for Administration
SUBJECT: Reassignment of Room Functions

A classroom has been lost to Central Scheduling, and this notification is to apprise you of the need in the future, commencing immediately, to replace that previously centrally scheduled facility with Room 113, Klutz Hall, which had hitherto been scheduled for use by the Department of Economics. Please so advise the department.

TO: Vice-President for Administration
FROM: Josef Martin, Dean of Arts and Sciences
SUBJECT: Loss of Classroom

I have recently found my own memory to be less reliable than it used to be, but I have never yet mislaid, let alone lost, anything approaching the magnitude of a classroom. Is there any way that Central Scheduling might, through recourse to files or plans of buildings, manage again to find the classroom it lost? So long as that possibility exists, I should not like to tell our economists that they no longer have a seminar room.

The V-P's memo had struck me as a fine example of the administrative use of the passive voice as a style of communicating, a mode that serves the sole purpose of disclaiming responsibility and is much used to that end.[6] It is useful, indeed important, to be clear about this. First, recognizing the device gives one the opportunity to attempt, as in my response to the V-P, not to let others get away with doing things without openly taking responsibility for them. If in the future they know that they might be flushed out of the passive voice, their actions might tend to become less reprehensible. (I cannot truthfully claim that it actually worked that way for me, but I still think it's worth trying.)

Second, and this I know to work, one can as necessary evade responsibility oneself by learning to write of one's own decisions in the passive voice. Deans only make trouble for themselves by writing, to chairs or to faculty, "I have decided . . . ," quite irrespective of *what* they may have decided; much better to write, "It has been decided . . . ," and thereby let the anger be directed at the university or at the central administration rather than at the dean individually and personally.

Notes

1. This is something that faculty know in principle but do not really understand, and which students have not the faintest glimmering of. (Indeed, not even the V-P seemed to realize that the dean of arts and sciences is the busiest person on campus—after only the president, who is rarely on campus. Having less time, incidentally, also ensures that the dean cannot plan and initiate grand ventures, and therefore he causes much less trouble than the V-P.)

Those who might think it fanciful that useful amounts of time can be saved by shortening one's style of signing should consult F. L. Wells and Helen R. Palwick, "Notes on Usage of Male Personal Names," *Journal of Social Psychology*, 31 (1950): 291–94. One reads there that the "present writer" shortened his style of signature in "World War I, when official duties required frequent affixings of signature." Please note that (1) the amount of paper circulated on campuses is comparable to the amount circulated in military organizations and therefore similar devices for saving time are appropriate in both; (2) the article referred to has two authors, but the quotation from it speaks of a single "writer"—was this not a fine way of making clear that the co-author's name was put on the piece only as an afterthought? What is not so clear is whether the senior author's attitude toward the co-author stemmed from the fact that the latter was a graduate student or that she was a woman. Either eventuality is plausible, of course, in the case of one who was a male adult as long ago as World War I.

I was occasionally embarrassed when a student referred to something I had signed, when the signing had actually been done by a machine trained to reproduce my signature: on diplomas or on letters congratulating those who had made the dean's list, for example. Only two students, out of many thousands who graduated while I was dean, have diplomas bearing my authentic signature: one, a friend of one of my daughters, has a diploma that I signed in person above the machine-written version; the other was a stranger to me, who brought me her diploma which had apparently been fed into the wrong machine, from which it emerged with the signature of the dean of architecture rather than that of the dean of arts and sciences.

2. My interpretations are much kinder than are those of the professional interpreters, however: "The child originally knows himself by his first name only. Knowledge of the last name does not develop until the age of three, on the average. . . . as persons grow older, they learn to think of themselves primarily in terms of their last name, and this may be an unconscious indicator of maturity" (A. A. Hartman, "Name Styles in Relation to Personality," *Journal of General Psychology,* 59 [1958]: 289–94).

Thus was it scientifically confirmed for me that "Pete T." had never matured much beyond the mental age of three. But even more far-reaching conclusions than that can be drawn from a person's choice of name-style:

John J. Doe—conformity

John Doe—also conformity, but greater frankness, directness, "or even some individuality"

John James Doe—narcissism, exhibitionism, exaggerated view of self; "in weak or passive individuals . . . an attempt to bolster oneself by a demonstrative display, particularly if the names are resounding"

J. J. Doe—restraint, emotional constriction, reserved, slight paranoid factor, wish to avoid revealing oneself; high energy, impatience, wish to present only essentials, dislike for unnecessary elaboration

J. Doe—self-derogatory, masochistic, negative self-feeling; feelings of unimportance, exaggerated modesty, casualness, wish to escape notice

J. James Doe—individualistic, narcissistic, striving for superiority

For further details, consult Hartman (above) or Wells and Palwick (note 1).

3. See chapter 9, "What It Takes."

4. The same point of course applies to the V-P and the P. If they allow faculty or students to gossip informally with them around and about chairs or deans, it soon becomes widely known that such behavior is acceptable to them; and that knowledge encourages more and more of the same. No neutrality is possible here. If the V-P does not express some degree of disbelief when a professor makes an allegation about a chair or a dean, the lack of a disbelieving response is inevitably taken as a sign of agreement.

A dean of my acquaintance served briefly with a V-P who didn't understand that. The V-P had an open door, practiced first-name interaction in person as well as in his memos, and would listen to anything without contradicting; moreover, he occasionally shared with members of the faculty some of his reservations about chairs and deans. To a request from a professor for funds for some special project, for instance, he might respond, "Why not ask the dean? He's a good fellow, though awfully tight with the purse strings. He's got a contingency fund of nearly half-a-million dollars that he just refuses to spend." And thus that V-P eroded the effectiveness of several chairs and more than one dean.

5. From the issue dated 15 September 1986: "The advertisement for the position of MATERIALS TECHNICIAN in the Center for Solid State Science at . . . which appeared in the Academic Positions Section of the August 18, 1986 issue of Chemical & Engineering News inadvertantly [*sic*] did not include the facts that . . . is an Affirmative Action/Equal Opportunity Employer and minorities are encouraged to apply. Application deadline extended to October 15, 1986 or until filled. Submit resume and 3 references to. . . ."

6. For a full and delightful discussion, see Richard Mitchell, *Less Than Words Can Say*, Boston & Toronto: Little, Brown, 1979.

6

What the Dean Wants

"You're the dean," he said to me with a conspiratorial half-smile. "You're the dean, and you can do anything you want."

Except, I thought to myself, anything that *you* don't want to see happen, in which case you'd be among the first to raise hell. Too bad I can't tell you that you've forfeited your right to an opinion by not standing up for it openly.

Alfred was a fairly senior full professor, expressing dismay that his departmental colleagues had recommended for tenure an obviously unqualified person. He came to tell me that I should oppose the recommendation. Of course, he himself had not openly pressed the case against tenure: "You know how it is," he confided; "the chairman is backing her, and I don't want to embarrass him, and anyway how can anybody oppose tenure for a woman?"

Yes, I acknowledged silently, I know how it is. You're afraid of the chairman, who can't seriously damage you and wouldn't if he could. I should be flattered, I suppose, that you don't regard me as being an "anybody" who can't oppose tenure for a woman.

* * * * *

I wished these things didn't happen: tenured full professors afraid to speak their minds; and faculty telling me that I should do something, without apparently pausing to consider that it might not be proper for me to do it.

Already as a faculty member and before my administrative stint, I had been dismayed by the cowardice among my colleagues. What did they fear? Attempted reprisals by a chair could be appealed in several ways. Apart from those safeguards, what would actually have been at risk? Perhaps part of a salary raise or a travel allowance? Not speaking one's mind on a significant academic issue, for fear of those sorts of possibilities, is like selling one's soul for a mess of pottage. Roosevelt knew: we have nothing to fear but fear itself. Professors have nothing to fear but themselves. What sad things does it indicate, that their fear is often so great?

*   *   *   *   *

In a sense, of course, any of us can do anything we want. Professors can say in class anything they want;[1] professors can talk in class about anything they want; professors can assign grades just as they want.

A coed once asked me to change her grade from C to B, otherwise her average would be too low to permit her to remain in her sorority: "And that's my whole life just now." Trying to find some common ground on which to build communication, I showed her that many other grades of C in her class were based on higher actual marks than hers. If I were to change her grade, then I would have to change all those others too.

"But why?" she asked in puzzlement. "Nobody would know."

In one way, I wished I could do what she so desperately wanted. She reminded me of my own children, if only because of her age, and I recognized the urgency assumed in those years by such—to me, now—irrelevancies as sororities. But even with my own children I was usually aware of the responsibility to act as a proper father: the responsibility not to succumb too readily to my emotions of love and empathy but to consider as coolly as I could what might better serve the best interests of those I loved. And I usually concluded that their interests were best served by learning principles and values, and, even more important, by learning to abide by those principles and values. I-the-professor couldn't possibly change that young woman's grade. Furthermore, it was my responsibility to try to make her understand why: because there were no proper grounds for doing so.

*   *   *   *   *

We can do anything we want, *provided, of course, that it is a proper thing to do.* That surely understood qualifying phrase had not, I feared, been in Professor Alfred's mind. I'm the dean, yes, but I can only do anything *that it is proper for a dean to want to do.* It is not necessarily proper for I-the-dean to do what I-the-man might want to do. For instance, like most people I have my own personal biases about which disciplines should thrive and which should wither away; but it would be improper for me to use my position as dean to those ends, since there is no consensus in academe or on my own campus on those matters. I simply have no warrant to use my position to such ends. It's difficult enough, perhaps impossible, not to let such personal biases influence subconsciously my decisions; being quite clear that they ought not to, however, is at least something of a safeguard.

I had observed since entering academe that professors are not always good at separating their personal biases from their proper academic roles. When strong ideological motives enter the picture, nuances important to academic freedom tend to get overlooked. Doesn't academic freedom mean that professors can talk in class about anything they want? No, indeed, it does not—not without a sorely needed qualifying phrase: professors can talk in class about anything they want *that is relevant to the courses they are teaching.* Many "liberals" forgot that qualifying phrase during the Vietnam-protest days, when personal conscience or duty to humankind or something of that sort was supposed to carry overriding weight. But professors are simply not entitled to use the professorial role to express personal convictions of that sort, no matter how strongly or sincerely held those convictions may be. For that sort of expression there is the street corner, the soap box, the letter to the newspaper, the voting booth. Academic freedom *does* ensure that professors do not risk their employment when they make appropriate citizenly use of those avenues of expression. *In the classroom,* however, the proper role of professors is restricted to that of exponents of their subjects. Professors must obey the dictates of conscience appropriate to scholars: their duty in the classroom is solely to serve the field of history, or chemistry, or whatever.

Our faculty senate once considered a motion that "with respect to the proposed nationwide remembrance of events at Kent State, the university should recognize the right of every member of the faculty to follow the dictates of her or his conscience." One of our feistier professors asked whether the motion was intended to protect people who canceled their classes in observance of the call for a national moratorium? Naturally he was not given an answer. "The motion means exactly what it says," was the brave response—revealing, it seemed to me, not only the standard unwillingness to stand up openly for one's opinion but also at least an inkling of an understanding that academic freedom really could not be stretched to cover the canceling of classes on such grounds. Needed in the motion, of course, was a modifying phrase: the right of every member of the faculty (as well as of everyone else, incidentally) to follow the dictates of conscience *and to accept the consequences*—a qualification that conscientious objectors understand, or at least did in the good old days.

*　　*　　*　　*　　*

It often seemed to me that I was alone in pondering what it might be proper for a dean to do. Professors and students would come to ask that I do certain things . . . but only because they themselves wanted them done. All too often they didn't seem to understand what I meant when I talked to them about proper procedure and about what a dean might or ought to do. That young coed certainly didn't understand when she had said, "No one would know," and I had replied, "But *I* would know."[2]

Most of the time, not the dean but the relevant department should make the decisions: about courses and programs; about hiring, tenuring, promoting, or dismissing; about how to divide the department's budget and the department's allotment for salary raises. The dean ought to be there just to keep the departments honest, to make them give good reasons for what they decide. Of course, that's not always understood either. "We know our business, don't you trust us?" they say. Well, most of the time, yes; but occasionally, no. When to trust and when not to trust is a question that deans must continually ask themselves.

Deans can only make judgments at one remove. They can learn about what is usual in the various disciplines: what work is prized and what is not, where the best departments in the field are, who the best people are. And, too, a dean can sometimes remind a department that it said something different on another occasion. One doesn't need a dean if the dean is always a rubber stamp. Ideally, a dean should always abide by decisions reached at the departmental level—but "ideally" includes that it be an ideal department in its field, that the professors in it be ideal professors in their field. And since that isn't always the case, at times the dean must say "No" and try to make happen what would happen in an ideal department.

Of course, you're damned if you don't as well as if you do. I once queried strenuously a recommendation for tenure from a reasonably strong department in which some of the best professors opposed (not openly, of course) the recommendation. But the chairman argued passionately for the candidate, and most of the faculty did too, and finally I concluded that their judgment was honest. I supported the case and it went through. Later I heard that one professor of the minority view had told the story to some people at another university: "weak dean" was the inevitable kibitzers' conclusion.

No dean, of course, can simply accept departmental judgments about the totals of budgets, salaries, or raises, for there is not nearly enough money to go around. Should the dean spread the available amounts "evenly," be egalitarian, or should excellence be sought in selected areas? Obviously the latter, everyone agrees, without (again obviously) agreeing what those selected areas should be. And the dean can't make openly plain what those areas are to be because the others would immediately be in revolt and their faculty in flight. So the dean must tell white lies.[3] Not, of course, to the vice-president, to whom the dean must justify what he does; but *complete* openness in that direction, too, would be a mistake. Vice-presidents have long memories for individuals or departments that a dean describes as other than outstanding, and those can become tempting reasons or rationalizations if the vice-president decides to cut the college's resources. So deciding among departments must be at least in part a lonely endeavor. It is one way deans may actually earn what they are paid.

In any case, what would "egalitarian" among departments actually look like in practice? Hire assistant professors of music at the same salary as computer scientists and see what happens? . . . Give the English department the same budget as the chemistry department, and then pack your briefcase? The nature of the discipline overrides all such purely quantitative guides as numbers of majors, numbers of students taught, numbers of faculty. What *is* an equitable distribution among thirty departments covering the range of arts and sciences? Finding out how it's done elsewhere might help . . . if you could find out. Some useful data on salaries are available,[4] but not on operating budgets.[5] So you use whatever you can get and what you can infer from local history and events. For instance, Department A is bankrupt by January whereas most of the others can pay their bills until March: clearly you didn't give Department A enough— unless, that is, A's chair is either fiscally incompetent or very competent indeed, having decided that this is the best strategy for getting a larger budget for the department next year. When you know your chairs well, you can try using that knowledge. Give the unreasonably insatiable ones much less than they ask and the conservative ones a little more than they ask: while that could well be the most objectively warranted approach, how-

ever, it will make them both unhappy. Or see how much each
department spent on travel. Since that's the first item they cut
if they're strapped, the least-dollars-per-faculty-member-for-
travel department is obviously the one you short-changed—unless, that is, some chair knows what you're doing and spends as
little as possible on travel this year in order to get a bonanza
next year.

*   *   *   *   *

We've digressed from Professor Alfred's myopia about propriety and other matters. He believes that deans are paid (far
too much, incidentally) to make the hard decisions, and this tenure case was one for me to earn my keep on.

Not only Alfred, of course, talks about "having the guts" to
make the "hard" decision. The decision is supposed to be hard,
let us be clear, because some people will not like it, not because
it is supposed to be hard in the sense of difficult to discern what
the right course of action is. Just as with the proprieties, I'm
puzzled that so few seem to be clear about that. Deans—and
professors and others too—are paid to do their jobs, which surely
means to do them right. If some people won't like you if you
do the job right, what should you do? Do the job wrong so that
you'll be liked, which means that you'll continue to have the
job and continue to do it badly? Is it more important to *have*
the job or to *do* the job?

Of course doing the job right is stressful; that's why there are
leaves, vacations, tranquilizers, and psychotherapists. Perhaps
the greatest stress, however, or the most difficult to treat, comes
from doing something that you know you shouldn't do. If you
are honestly of the opinion that your decision is right, and if
you are clear about the reasons, you can find ways to ease the
stress occasioned by the unreasonable or excessive hostility of
those you've displeased. But do what you know to be the wrong
thing, just to avoid hostility, and after a while you won't like
yourself at all—and you'll be disappointed to find that you have
still aroused hostility, albeit from other directions.

Admittedly there is no objective or consensual right or wrong in most of these matters. But before you were chosen to be dean, you were interviewed and you expressed opinions about education and administration and what a college ought to be and what a dean should do and how. Presumably you were chosen at least in part because of those opinions. So doing the right thing could minimally mean being faithful to the opinions and ideals you expressed earlier—in a sense, they form an implicit contract, just as professors are told to view their syllabi as contracts with their students.

*   *   *   *   *

As it happened, I thought that Professor Alfred had been right to oppose tenure on that occasion. Sufficiently many others thought so too, and the department was overruled and tenure was denied. I've sometimes wondered whether Alfred gave himself much credit for that. Did he believe that I had needed his counsel to evaluate properly the merits of the case? Did he think I had done what he asked rather than what I deemed right?

Notes

1. A professor's communication with students may also, of course, proceed via nonverbal channels. One of our chairs needed to see me on short notice. "You may find this a bit hard to believe," he said, "but Gaither has just thrown a full garbage can at a student."

I've had the impulse myself at times, I thought. "How great was the provocation?" I asked. "Had the student just barged into Gaither's office and made some impossible demand in a boorish way?"

"Oh, it wasn't in Gaither's office, it was during class."

Good God, I thought, we are to be spared nothing. "Well, what had the student done?"

"It seems that she asked, 'What is Zen?' "

*   *   *   *   *

Gaither later insisted that he had merely inverted the trash can and placed it on the student's desk—it was simply an unfortunate accident that there happened to be some rubbish in it which soiled the desk and the student's clothes. "Everyone knows," he said, "that you can't explain in words what Zen is." The student's father, as it happened, didn't know that and was not prepared to concede that academic freedom could cover such instances of nonverbal communication. I agreed with him, I must say, and would have done so even if he had not happened to be one of the university's most consistent and generous benefactors.

*   *   *   *   *

I must add that, no matter the particular subject, what everyone knows is much more likely to be wrong than to be right. That is, when someone tells me a thing and I ask for proof and all I get is "everyone knows . . . ," then I feel comfortably able to shrug it off; if that assertion is the best evidence available, then I need not apologize for remaining unconvinced. "Everyone knows," after all, that Richard III murdered his nephews to gain the throne; "everyone knows" that the Loch Ness Monster is but a myth; not so long ago, "everyone knew" that the healthiest state was to be a little underweight, but nowadays "everyone knows" that it is better to be just slightly overweight.

Thus, too, "everyone knows" that universities harbor incompetent professors protected by tenure. As dean, I found that not only outsiders knew that but some students did too—especially those who were chosen to sit on student affairs committees and governing boards—and also some faculty and some vice-presidents. To all and sundry who said it in my presence, I responded quite impatiently: give me the names of the individuals of whom you speak, and give me the prima facie evidence, and I will investigate; and if you turn out to be right, I assure you that I will act, by giving low salary raises or none at all; and I'm quite prepared to go as far as instituting proceedings for dismissal for cause if that seems warranted.

Not once was my challenge taken up. Rather, and invariably, I would be told—perhaps together with a good-humored dig to the ribs— "Come on, now! You can level with me. You know as well as I do that it's true. But the students are afraid to say anything about any instructor, and the faculty protect one another, and the administrators wouldn't do anything anyway. Everyone knows that. . . ."

As it happens, I don't know that; in fact, I happen to know the opposite. I've known a number of people who were unpopular with students for various reasons—bitchy personality, or tentative and shy and retiring, or somewhat disorganized—but only when the moon was blue did I come across an instructor who was demonstrably *incompetent*—

that is, so unknowledgeable about a subject as to have been unable to help others learn it. The most unpopular instructors, about whom we got complaints year after year, always had some very strong supporters among the students and the faculty.

I venture to say that the proportion of incompetents among professors is lower than the proportion of incompetents in other professions. The fact is that no other occupation subjects its members to as long and rigorous an apprenticeship as does academe; and no other occupation rejects as large a proportion of its neophytes. One's first faculty appointment offers a *maximum* of seven years' employment unless one performs so well that tenure is offered before then. I have found no reliable national statistics, but my own experience indicates that only about one-third or one-half of the people who get a tenure-track appointment eventually attain tenure in the same institution. In what other profession do only one-third or one-half of those *who are initially well qualified for a position* attain permanence in it? Do we reject as many as a half of those who begin careers in law or in medicine? What everyone *should* know is that professors are outstandingly educated, rigorously selected, and uncommonly conscientious.

2. Two of my senior colleagues have several times taught a popular course about the Arthurian legends. They find that the students have great difficulty in understanding the knights' code. In particular, the students do not understand why the loser of a joust, after having given his word to the victor, actually does travel—though unaccompanied—to Arthur's court to swear allegiance. I find it genuinely horrifying that our culture apparently now fails to transmit the tradition or the ethic that one's word is one's bond.

3. That aspect of deaning, together with the university's traditional mission of seeking scholarly truth, led one of my colleagues to suggest that the dean's motto ought to be "Truth is our profession" (by analogy with the Strategic Air Command, which proclaims "Peace is our profession"). Another of my colleagues addressed the same issue by reminding everyone frequently that a dean must always stand ready to rise above principle.

4. The Office of Institutional Research at Oklahoma State University publishes annually a summary of average salaries for each rank in each discipline. Sadly lacking, however, are data on the relationship between salary and time in rank or age or professional seniority. For chemistry and for statistics, information of that sort is available from

the professional societies; but it is not safe to assume that the same trends apply to all disciplines. Thus the pecking order of starting salaries changes dramatically over the course of but a few years, and that of upper-level salaries only slightly less quickly.

5. I had really detailed information about two colleges only and somewhat less reliable and less detailed data from annual surveys of another dozen. Those data, however, support the following generalities:

> No more than 85 percent of the total budget should be needed for salaries and wages. Of that payroll, at least 20 percent should be for secretarial, technical, and professional staff to provide support to the faculty. Of the operating part of the budget, at least 25 percent should be available to maintain and replace major equipment.
>
> In practice, however, the payroll is often 90 percent or more of the college's total budget (I heard from deans who suffered at 95 percent and more), there are rarely enough supporting staff, and major equipment is often purchased only in bonanza years.

Those figures are for the college as a whole, of course, and must be varied somewhat according to the mix of arts and sciences (expensive in both equipment and operations) to letters and social sciences (relatively inexpensive). For the university as a whole, the payroll is a much smaller part of the total budget, largely because of all the non-academic things that are paid for centrally.

7

The Law

"I think we should give them whatever they ask for," said our university attorney. "We certainly don't want the EEO people to think we're not being cooperative."

Oh my God, I thought, here we go again. Doesn't anyone realize that the requests will become ever more irrelevant, time-consuming, intolerable, unless we insist that a rational case be made for them? Does even our own attorney believe that we have something to fear even where we have done no wrong?

"Please," I said, "two points. First, if we hand over the stuff we are implicitly agreeing that it's relevant, and we shouldn't, we mustn't do that. Second, to get all the material together will be a considerable burden on all of our chairs and I won't permit that if it isn't absolutely necessary."

Naturally I was overruled.

The plaintiff had held a one-year visiting appointment, clearly described as such in the letter of appointment. During that year, the department had advertised a tenure-track vacancy, but it was not in the plaintiff's subspecialty, her teaching was not very impressive, and so she had not been short-listed for a formal interview. She had then charged sex discrimination, had received no satisfaction through the university's procedures for handling such complaints, and had gone to the Feds. They wanted from the university the following: for the last six years, a list of every person—identified by sex and ethnic classification as well as name—who had held a temporary appointment, not merely in the plaintiff's department but in every department in the university; a list of all the tenure-track vacancies advertised during those six years; a list of all the temporary employees who had been interviewed for those positions and, if they had not been appointed, the reasons for that; a list of reasons why the others had not been interviewed, together with their vitae and the vitae of the people who *had* been interviewed; and no doubt some other items as well, which I have mercifully forgotten in the meantime.

*   *   *   *   *

Everyone seemed to take for granted that the denial of tenure or even the denial of an initial appointment to a female candidate was likely to result in legal action. During my time as dean, several men took recourse to legal procedures, but that was rarely talked about; the conventional wisdom was that only women were doing this, and that all rejected women did so. Now it is true that more women took us to court than did men; and certainly a much higher proportion of the unsuccessful women than of the unsuccessful men took that route. Never obvious to the conventional wisdom, however, was the significant number of capable women who never made any fuss or threat and who were quietly appointed and tenured and promoted solely on account of their abilities and achievements.

It is also true, though, that as dean I saw few furies like some of the women scorned for tenure. I came to believe that these women—very small in number but oh, so visible—had long ago acquired the absolute conviction that women would never and could never get a fair shake. When tenure was then actually denied them, the long and partly suppressed fury of many years found a definite focus for expression, and the explosion was much more violent than in the case of the denied males, for whom it was a personal set-back but not in addition an ideological one.

Some such explanation as this is needed, it seems to me, for the extremity of passion and lack of logic, indeed of plain common sense, evinced by these complainants. They simply could not grasp that, to others, the denial of tenure to them was not obvious proof that sex discrimination was being routinely practiced. Apparently they gave no moment's thought to the other women, the successful ones who were being tenured and promoted all the time: why hadn't we discriminated against them? If the answer was that *those* had been obviously clear-cut cases, then it would of course be admitted that the ones denied had *not* been clear-cut. Since our university had long said explicitly that doubtful cases were to be resolved against the candidate, gender unspecified, it was difficult to see as evidence of sex discrimination that women without clear-cut credentials were denied tenured appointments.

Facts and logic notwithstanding, however, our faculty and chairs and administration and attorney were all convinced that, in the climate of the times, though the onus might well be on male candidates to prove their worth, with female candidates the onus was on the university to prove that they did *not* have the necessary credentials—not even the necessary "minimum" credentials, whatever sense "minimum" might make in the context of our stated mission of pursuing excellence. Our attorney routinely recommended that we reach whatever settlement we could out of court, the merits of the actual case quite notwithstanding. That led in one instance to a conclusion that I offer as quite possibly unique.

*   *   *   *   *

"Please wait until I've finished saying what I'm about to say," the vice-president pleaded, projecting charm and sincerity as only he could. "Please don't jump to conclusions or get upset before I've given you the whole picture, and I'm sure you'll find it, on reflection, quite acceptable."

With that preamble, I thought, he's surely going to come out with something that I very definitely *ought* to refuse to go along with. Surely they can't seriously be considering giving her tenure?

The plaintiff had not been recommended for tenure by her department. She had appealed to me, then to the vice-president, then to the several available committees; obtaining no satisfaction, she had hired a lawyer to press the charge of sex discrimination.

"I'll try to be reasonable," I said to the V-P, meaning precisely that. "Go ahead."

"Well," he continued, "her lawyer has written to the president that they will sue for damages unless he writes a letter awarding her tenure. Of course, the president is not questioning the correctness of the decision not to tenure, and in no way would he want to imply lack of trust in the department's recommendation or in the college's or in yours; but the university attorney is strongly recommending that we settle out of court if we feel at all able to, to save untold amounts of time for many people and also sizable costs even though we would win the case. Now, you know that Ms. Brown has already taken a job at another university, she isn't here any longer, and so it's hard to see what damage would be done if the president did write a letter awarding her tenure here."

I counted to fifteen, as I remember, to be quite on the safe side, and tried to simulate the behavior of a loyal member of the administrative team.

"I do feel for the president, on many other things as well as on this; and I think I understand that he needs to rely on the advice of the attorney about legal matters. But how could such a letter from him *not* imply a lack of trust in our recommendations? More important, perhaps, and please excuse my growing paranoia, but I'm not really inclined to trust Ms. Brown's motives. How do we know that she will not come back here if she gets a letter awarding her tenure? Is she so happy in her new job? If so, why hasn't she dropped the suit?"

The V-P nodded, calm and businesslike, evidently relieved that my voice had not been raised to an undue degree. "Very good points, and they had also occurred to us. In point of fact, if the president gives Ms. Brown a letter awarding her tenure then she will give him a letter pledging not to return here and never to apply for a position here in the future."

At last, I thought, I can quite safely say that now I've heard everything and will not ever again be surprised at what life brings to a dean.

"You really mean," I asked, "that she will say in writing that she will not return, that she will drop her suit, and will never apply for a job here, if the president awards her tenure? Then what good is that bit of paper to her? What does a letter of tenure mean without the substance of tenure?"

"Well," the V-P said, less emphatically and with more uncertainty than was his wont, "I can't of course pretend to understand it myself. She says she just wants the vindication for her own satisfaction."

"I do find it hard to imagine what satisfaction that could be," I mused. "Could we be overlooking something? What about her promise not to return—could she be held to that? Isn't there something in the Constitution that citizens cannot sign away their rights, willingly or not? Perhaps even her written pledge would not be legally binding?"

"Excellent point," responded the V-P. "You're as sharp and logical and thoughtful as ever." (Oh dear, I told myself, all those compliments mean that he really is quite determined to get my agreement.) "Yes, we did quiz our attorney quite carefully on that one, and he is quite sure that an agreement can be drafted that will be quite legally binding on all parties."

"Oh," I asked in some surprise, "you mean there wouldn't just be an exchange of letters, there would first be a written agreement to make such an exchange?"

"Why of course," said the V-P, who was now clearly less sure of the sharpness of my wits. "Oh, naturally, we would have to know that we were completely covered before having the president write a letter of tenure."

"So we would have in writing," I reiterated, "signed by Ms. Brown and by her lawyer, an implicit acknowledgment that we were blackmailed into granting her tenure, on the understanding however—to which she willingly would agree—that she would never take up the tenured appointment?"

"Some people might view it like that," the V-P smiled, trying unsuccessfully not to look smug. "We think it would be an excellent deal for us, to avoid the expense involved in court action, not to mention the waste of time for all the people who would have to appear, not only the president but of course you and me and so on. But the president does want me to assure you that we don't want to do anything that you couldn't live with."

Again a bind that I had experienced before. Somehow I found myself in a situation where doing the principled thing would seem like being unprincipled, disloyal, and downright unreasonable; in short, behaving more like a faculty member than like a member of the administrative team.

"There has to be a flaw somewhere," I mused. "Who would be allowed access to that agreement? I assume it would be confidential to the signatories. Now suppose Ms. Brown wants to get early tenure in her new job and she shows them the letter from our president granting her tenure here, as a way of making them hurry up; then they likely have the sense to call me to ask about her—do I have to lie? What would I say?"

"No," assured the V-P, "you would be free to tell the truth; we all would be. There is to be no provision for the agreement to be held secret or even confidential. Ms. Brown says she just wants the satisfaction of an official letter vindicating her own belief that she should have been granted tenure here."

"I really don't want to seem slow or stupid," I said, "but let me just see whether I understand properly. There will be an agreement, signed by people from here and by Ms. Brown, saying she will drop all legal actions against us and write us a letter pledging not to take up her tenure here, now or ever in the future; in return, the president gives her what is patently an entirely worthless letter saying she has tenure here, totally meaningless since tenure has no significance if one doesn't have a position into which to be tenured; *and* I am free to tell the world about this?''

"That's about it," nodded the V-P, exuding his usual self-assurance and confidence, now that he sensed I was hooked. "Of course, you probably should not go around trumpeting unasked that Ms. Brown blackmailed us—if only because that is an interpretation rather than a demonstrable fact. But there is no confidentiality asked for with respect to the facts, and the agreement will state specifically that we can respond truthfully to inquiries directed to us about the award of tenure to Ms. Brown."

"I really don't want to be difficult," I said, "and obviously I must go along on the basis you've outlined, if the president really believes that's best. I just wish that sometime or other we would call one of these bluffs, and go to court, and make mincemeat of them, and thereafter remind future nuisances that we can and do win and won't be pushed around when we haven't set a foot wrong. And I must admit that I'm still a little bothered by the implication that the president overrules all the internal recommendations against tenure. Do you think he might perhaps write yet another letter, perhaps to me, expressing full trust in the procedures by which the college makes these recommendations and in the integrity of the people involved?"

"Oh, absolutely, good idea, I'm sure he will *want* to do that, he'll be grateful for the reminder." The V-P smiled broadly as he stood up. I got up too, and he shook my hand and patted me on the shoulder. "I knew we could rely on you to be reasonable and to cooperate."

You knew no such thing, I thought, as your ample relief and profuse compliments to me demonstrate. Have I really now compromised something that I shouldn't have? What possible harm can this do so long as the truth can be told?

*   *   *   *   *

So the agreement was consummated, and several weeks later the exchange of letters was effected. I joked about that with the V-P: I pictured the impending event as resembling one of those movie scenes in which a kidnap victim is ransomed, or East and West exchange captured spies. The two sides, each unable to trust the other even for a moment, are separated by a stretch of neutral ground. Slowly, one person from each side steps forward, holding one of the crucial letters; the two advance further, stopping when they are a pace apart, each holding up the letter so that the other can read it. When both are satisfied, they extend their hands and grasp the two letters simultaneously; then they release their grasp on the ones to be released and slowly step backward out of range, finally turning and scurrying back to their companions.

I don't know whether the actual scene was like that because I wasn't there. And I still cannot understand what satisfaction it could have brought Ms. Brown, though it evidently did: our attorney claims that she brought along a bottle of champagne to celebrate the exchange of letters.

8

A Personal Question

"Can I ask you a personal question?" he ventured after a while.

"Of course," I replied automatically.

Clasper had been denied tenure the previous year. In accord with normal practice, he had been given a contract for the current year on the clear understanding that it would be his last term of employment on our faculty. Now he wanted again to be considered for possible tenure, because several more articles under his name had been published in the meantime. I had been explaining to him—or trying to—that we didn't do things that way. Everyone was assessed for tenure at the latest during the sixth year of service, essentially on the record of five full years of teaching and scholarship. Evaluating Clasper during his seventh year would hardly be equitable to all the others who had been evaluated during their sixth; most everyone, after all, could produce a few more articles in another year. Besides, I told him, we hadn't just counted how many papers he had published: we had solicited opinions about the significance of his work from qualified senior people at other universities. Another few articles of the same sort as his earlier ones would hardly make the needed difference. No, I said, the rules don't permit reconsideration now, and there are sound reasons for the rules.

So then he said he wanted to ask a personal question, and I automatically told him to go ahead. Automatically because I had decided long before that I should always do what I could to ease the strain that denial of tenure brings; and what little I could do included listening, and letting the disappointed ones work off their anger and talk through their anxieties, and responding to what they said, and even letting them ask personal questions.

I tried always to be firm about the decision on tenure but sympathetic to personal circumstances. I was usually met by surprise when, in the course of these conversations, I would say, "Don't confuse matters by questioning the justice or equity of the decision. Look at it realistically, as a decision reached after several independent recommendations by committees and individuals. Like all human judgments, it's fallible. But we have so elaborated the procedures and avenues for appeal that everything that could be said, has been said. It is proper *procedure* that determines whether there has been justice or equity; people will often, perhaps always, disagree about whether a given *decision* was right or wrong, but it has to be made somehow, and it is the *procedures* that make for equity or inequity. It's just the same with judicial or political processes: we take pride in our democratic way of doing things as being the fair way, without claiming that every result is therefore the right, just, or equitable one. You are quite free to believe that the decision is wrong, and perhaps you can make a successful career elsewhere and thereby prove us wrong. Don't take our decision as a judgment of your inherent abilities, let alone as a judgment of you as a person. It is simply that, at this time, your achievements don't fit with what this university believes appropriate for making the offer of a tenured appointment."

I hardly ever knew whether such comments helped or whether it would have been better just to let the anger be vented on me. I suspect that most of those who were ready to come to terms with the decision didn't bother to come to talk with me, and that most of those who came in were in no mood to hear what I said. Certainly on this occasion I saw no lessening of the anger.

Clasper was in any case an angry young man—though not quite as young as he was angry, and not quite as young as he looked, dressed, and behaved. He had been in college during the Student Revolt Against Reality, and his views had hardly changed since then. He wore work clothes and hiking boots (which, I thought, must have been quite uncomfortable during the warmer weather); when the temperatures were really high, he sometimes sported shorts and sandals, naturally without socks (which I thought must have been equally uncomfortable in the air-conditioned buildings). He was quite aggressively informal: I recall a seminar by a visiting eminence, during which Clasper sat—or rather sprawled—on the floor, and not for want of chairs, since there were a number not occupied. He took part in the discussion without bothering to rise, and I remember hoping that our visitor had taken him for a student rather than for a member of the faculty.

Well, he wanted to ask a personal question, and that's what I get paid for, among other things.

"Are you a European Jew?" was Clasper's personal question. Personal indeed, and a new one on me.

"Yes," I replied, and wondered whether it was just curiosity on his part, and if so what that might mean. What on earth could be the point, the relevance to his situation?

"Well," he said, and his manner now indicated that he had a telling point to make. He had begun to speak again just as soon as I had answered; evidently he had known the answer and had planned exactly what he was going to say next. "Well, considering the Holocaust and all that happened in Nazi Germany because people followed orders, how can you be such a stickler for the rules?"

Ah, I thought, now, once again, I've heard everything and will never be surprised by anything hereafter. Where can I begin, what can I hope to accomplish when such a total reeducation is apparently needed? Should I address first the presumption that following rules must always be bad? Was he really an anarchist, or was it only the rules of others that he believed one should not follow? Didn't he expect his students or his family to abide by some rules? Or should one have rules but make a point of breaking them, capriciously and often, to demonstrate one's freedom or individuality or nonfascist character? At any rate, I had to grant that such misguided notions would be consistent with the general impression he gave, that he had not moved beyond the incoherent views of the student revolutionaries.

Without rules, or without consistent application of rules, how did he imagine that there could be fairness, or equity, or law, or civilization? Could we really "cut through all the junk" and instinctively know what is right and fair in every circumstance? Where would such instincts stem from, and how would they have been formed? From his own example, how would we have been morally equipped to deal with such as the Nazis, in the absence of our commitment to a society of orderliness, of rules based on principles and values?

What, I wondered (and not for the first time), gives these brash young upstarts the confident belief that they have something worth saying, and a right to be listened to, and a right to influence decisions? They have not yet done anything: they haven't produced scholarship found interesting by others; in the classroom, they voice uncritically the slogans of others, the fads of their student days; they haven't even experienced much of everyday life. They seem to have retained the narcissism of infancy, the conviction that the world owes them gratification. Should every angry young man be his own judge for tenure?

Could Clasper, I wondered, allow himself to discriminate on intellectual grounds among any collection of ideas in general, and in particular between different sorts of rules? The following of orders in Nazi Germany had been abhorrent precisely because those orders were not based on general rules informed by civilized principles and values. The Leader's word had been the Law; and all the Sub-Leaders could lay down Sub-Laws to their underlings. The orders were personal and thus capricious; and in the absence of governing principles there was also no accountability. Those officials could indeed—*pace* Professor Alfred—do what they wanted, whether or not it might be proper for them to do so. No such notion of propriety existed for them; they were free to do as they wanted, to use their power of office to do what, for purely personal reasons, they wanted to do.

In point of fact, I believe that in significant part my experience and understanding of the Nazi phenomenon led me to value *orderly* authority under rules that recognize as germane only criteria that are directly relevant to the particular issue at hand. As a Jewish child, I was ejected from the public schools; yet what relevance does ancestry have to public, secular education? And it is my understanding of the Nazi phenomenon that led me to realize that individuals can enjoy rights only when they are not regarded as members of groups or classes. There, ultimately, is the flaw in "affirmative action": that the state decrees that blacks and women and others shall be treated not as individuals but as members of classes.[1]

What conceivable analogy could Clasper see between the totalitarian and corrupt anarchy of Nazi Germany and our system of rules governed by principles and evolved after lengthy and open discussion leading to consensus? Should I-the-dean have had the warrant to cut across all the rules and procedural safeguards whenever it seemed good to me for personal reasons? Or only when I was asked to do so by a self-interested and angry young man? On what basis could I then be accountable, and to whom? To a town meeting of students and angry young faculty, perhaps?

I did my best to hold in check my anger and incredulity and depth of feeling, but I doubt that Clasper understood anything I said. I'm still not sure whether he had actually hoped that his line of argument could sway me, or whether he had just wanted to lash out and hurt me. Probably the latter; and perhaps his question revealed how deeply he himself hurt, even without knowing it. Not for the first time I grieved for the Claspers who made it through primary school and secondary school and college and graduate school without learning much about the world, about history, about themselves, about logic or hard thinking, about the satisfactions that can come from scholarly work. All we could do now was not to tenure them. What a waste and what a pity.

Note

1. Activist groups also damage their own causes when they take up the cudgels for someone only because that person happens to belong to a particular group. When the women's groups fight for tenure for a mediocre woman, for instance, they make it easy for their opponents ever thereafter to discredit them quite plausibly. For words of uncommon sense about these and related matters, see Arnold Beichman, *Nine Lies about America*, New York: Pocket Books, 1973; Midge Decter, *The New Chastity and Other Arguments against Women's Liberation*, New York: Coward, McCann & Geoghegan, 1972; Nathan Glazer, *Affirmative Discrimination: Ethnic Inequality and Public Policy*, New York: Basic Books, 1975; Thomas Sowell, *Affirmative Action Reconsidered: Was It Necessary in Academia?*, Washington, D.C.: American Enterprise Institute, 1975; Professor X, *The Sociology of the Absurd*, New York: Simon & Schuster, 1970.

9

What It Takes

"What exactly do I need to do to get tenure?" I used to be asked with appalling frequency. And I found it equally appalling that so many already tenured faculty thought it a good question for the untenured to ask. We had accumulated a half-inch stack of material that was given to newly appointed faculty to explain and illustrate the procedures, criteria, and standards; we held panel discussions about those things, the local AAUP held more discussions, and the various women's groups held yet more. And still it was a rare meeting for me with a departmental faculty when the question did not come up.

To the untenured, individually or en masse, I would explicate truthfully and as best I could: teach conscientiously with due consideration for your students, establishing rapport with them and making them learn; publish a normal amount for your field, things that people of recognized distinction will judge worth doing and well done; and be a reliable colleague and do your share of the committee work.

"What *is* the normal amount of published work?" the questions would continue. "Does it matter whether it's a book or a series of articles? Does the stature of the journal matter very much? Is it good or bad to have co-authors? What about papers read at conferences? How about invited seminars? How much do grants count?'' There was no end to it.

Though I always tried to answer accurately and truthfully, to the untenured I never revealed the *whole* truth as I saw it, namely, that the surest path to tenure is trod by those who don't ask the question, those who feel no need to ask the question, those to whom the question simply does not occur.

*   *   *   *   *

I cannot comprehend what attraction university life appears to hold for those who don't, for their own sake, need a life of productive activity in a field that has fatally fascinated them. How can one bear to teach if one doesn't find the subject infinitely interesting? How can one keep courses and lectures up to date if one is not immersed in the happenings of the field? How can one do research unless one has no inner choice but to do it?

Learning and thinking need to be largely their own reward—the very considerable reward in academe being the opportunity to communicate one's learning and thinking to others who share one's own interests. If, in fact, one cannot do other than learn and think, then it is surely natural also to want to share one's thought with others. One must *want* to teach; one must *want* to publish.

I never could understand the talk or complaint about the pressure and the burden on faculty to publish. It seems to me a privilege to be in an environment where one is not just permitted to publish but is actually encouraged to do so, and often helped materially with secretaries, photocopying facilities, library services, costs of postage, and even the subventions often requested by many academic publishers. I just can't imagine what it would be like *not* to want to write, *not* to want to share ideas with others. What possible attraction can academe have for people who don't want to do those things? None of the tangible appurtenances of academic life are so attractive, surely: the pay is not high, and in some fields it can be miserably low; the prestige is not particularly great; and it can't be the long vacations, because you use them either for the writing that you must do or to earn the extra money that you think you need.

Surely most of the people who asked me all those questions about tenure did somehow share my own love for scholarship and for teaching. That they had been selected for appointment to our faculty meant that they had done exceptionally well in their studies, that they had shown every indication of high ability and aptitude for their subjects. Why, then, were they so very unsure of that ability and aptitude?

My guess is that David Riesman was all too horribly correct in describing the "other-directed" person and in seeing our society as increasingly producing such persons—or, more correctly, such nonpersons. To recall Riesman's descriptions briefly:[1] The inner-directed person has incorporated into ego and conscience a set of principles and values that serve as yardsticks of some stability, against which to measure whether what he contemplates or does is good, right, or valuable. The other-directed person, by contrast, lacks inner standards and looks continually to others, to the societal environment, to define what is good, right, or valuable—and so he is at the mercy of fads and fashions and can never be sure beforehand whether a thing will seem, *even to himself*, to be worthwhile. The other-directed person doesn't know whether he has done anything, or what, until he receives the opinions of others. To such people, of course, the gauntlet run toward tenure must seem Kafkaesque: they themselves don't have any stable criteria or standards or principles or values, and so of course they assume that no one else does either, that decisions about tenure are capriciously based on grounds that change from instant to instant.

I used to imagine, before I was dean, that the disciplines themselves must afford some stable criteria; but I came to learn that I had been naive about that also, or at least that the generalization does not hold across the board. In the natural sciences and in mathematics and in statistics, the accumulated corpus of knowledge, that is, the products of earlier research, do define rather clearly what is sound or useful; and, in point of fact, the

untenured faculty in those departments rarely asked what it took
to get tenure.[2] In most of the humanities and in some of the
social sciences, however, little is consensually agreed about what
makes work good or valuable. That is true, of course, in the arts
too, but it is also well understood by those faculty—they know
what is involved in reaching aesthetic judgments and why there
are differences of opinion over those, and I wasn't quizzed much
by them about how to get tenure. The endless questioning and
evident insecurity I encountered chiefly in the humanities and
in the social sciences.

"Why do you ask *me* these questions?" I wanted to say but
rarely did. "*You* ought to know how a book is received in your
field by contrast with a series of articles. *You* ought to know how
the quality of what you write will be judged by your peers, and
how they measure the status of journals, and how much prestige
comes with grants. . . ."

*   *   *   *   *

I was educated in the good old days, when people were educated to be inner-directed. It is only quite recently that I have
come to realize how much I owe to that mode of education: the
ability to be alone with myself without discomfort; the ability
to think difficult things through for myself; the confidence that—
within the obvious limits—I can manage and plan my life.

Not that I want to claim a high degree of self-confidence or
self-esteem. The confidence is merely that I know what the score
is, what the important factors are that determine events; that I
have a good sense of how other people view various matters;
that I understand well enough what is happening around me,
so that I can rather easily work out what I need to do to fit in
(if that's what I want to do). My *personal* self-confidence is not
particularly high. That I've published much has never seemed
to me grounds for self-congratulation; it's part of the job, and
I'm perennially surprised when I realize that the volume of my
work is significantly greater than that of most of my colleagues.
That some of my work has been judged good has also not seemed
to me grounds for self-congratulation, because there is little of

it that might be nominated as great and none that would be awarded that appellation if nominated. Not that I am claiming great modesty either. It is just that I have learned to look *with the eye of the discipline* at my own work as well as that of others, which means making comparisons with the greatest names in the history and the present of my field. Anything short of their accomplishments remains unquestionably short of their accomplishments.

The point, however, is that I have acquired a fairly stable and realistic sense of what counts and what does not, so that I can also be somewhat realistic about my own part and place in things. That does provide a sense of security, though it's not the same as a sense of personal self-confidence. I've seen my activities as being the natural activities of someone working in my field, and so I've hardly been inclined to take *personal* credit for things that went well. I maintained that habit of mind after becoming dean, and so was always surprised when I was complimented on something that seemed to me natural, for instance, expressing myself well in writing or in speech. Occasionally, when so complimented, I've dreamed of making a speech, to faculty and to administrators and to students:

"If you're sincere in your compliments, why don't you do likewise, or at least offer more opportunity for others to do likewise?

"Let me reveal a secret: I wasn't born this way, with the skills for which you compliment me. If I express myself better than do many of you, it is not because I was born doing that but because I've read a great deal, much of it worth reading, and because I've had a lot of practice in writing—and because I know I could write better and keep trying to learn to do so. I have a decent amount of general knowledge again because I've read a great deal, some of it not necessarily worth reading, and because I was taught to pay attention. I argue fairly well because I learned how to express myself and because I've done a lot of thinking and because I came to enjoy thinking; I know to look for ways of discriminating, and I know to relate particularities

with generalities. I appear to be consistent because I hold some
general principles and because I see relationships and patterns,
and because it is more important to me to do the right thing
than the popular thing—and please don't tell me I have the guts
to do the right thing, or the 'hard' thing; it is actually that I *don't*
have the guts *not* to do what appears to be right, I'm too afraid
of what I would think of myself otherwise.

"If you're sincere in your compliments, why don't you put
your money where your words are? I wasn't born this way, and
I can't even take credit for becoming this way. I was taught by
parents and by teachers that it is good and proper and useful,
indeed valuable, to pay attention, to study, to write, and to learn
about solid stuff. In high school I had several years each of English, French, German, and Latin; of general science, chemistry,
and physics; of various mathematics, of geography, of history.
I was short-changed in art and music, which I've regretted; and
I was not exposed to business, consumer relations, home economics, local government, social studies, or other such things,
which I've never regretted for a moment—indeed, I'm glad to
have missed the distractions.

"I would be very different now if I had been educated in some
other way. Surely I'd be much the poorer a person. Your compliments indicate that you approve of the results of my education. So why don't you do what is necessary to again produce
such results?

"If you're sincere about civil rights and about equal opportunity, give all kids a chance to be educated as we were. Sur-
round them with people who think that education is a marvelous
thing; expose them to people who find thinking to be fun. Maybe
they won't all grow up to be university administrators, but why
should they all want to? Don't you think the same skills are helpful no matter how one earns one's living or how one spends one's
time? I enjoy thinking and reading and discussing and writing,
and those are things that anyone can do, and that anyone can
get fun out of—if they've been taught right early enough. I'm
not suggesting that we should educate everyone well so that

everyone can get certain jobs. I'm suggesting we educate everybody well so that they can live enjoyably.

"As with so many of the things I want to say, I find here that Jacques Barzun expressed it better long ago: 'The reason teaching has to go on is that children are not born human; they are made so.' And I believe we should never say, 'Now I'm human enough and can stop learning.' We can each of us benefit from more education than we now have.

"One of the things I like about being dean of arts and sciences is that it is quite appropriate for me to preach like this. We stand for education, in contrast to vocational training. Why, I'm asked, get a general degree rather than one in business or in engineering? Because education should be for life and to make living enjoyable, not to quickly get ready for a job, to earn as much money as possible without having any idea how to enjoy what money makes perhaps more possible. The arts, the humanities, and the sciences deal with matters of permanent value, and if you don't begin to learn about them early, then you may never do so; the ephemeral stuff you might require for a specific job, you can always pick up if and when you need to. Major in English and learn to express yourself, major in philosophy and learn how to think, and I wager you can get most any job for which a bachelor's degree is a standard qualification—you'll beat out most business and other 'professional' graduates by a mile.

"A friend of mine recently visited a former professor who, at age ninety-six, was not very active physically. 'I imagine you get bored at times?' my friend asked. 'Nonsense!' came the reply. 'I can never be bored. Don't forget that I had a liberal-arts education.' "

*   *   *   *   *

On occasion, I actually took the opportunity to say some of these things, especially about the value of a "liberal" (that is, proper) education in contrast to "professional" (that is, vocational) undergraduate work. I would point out that, while we often pay lip service to the notion that "money isn't everything," we still encourage youngsters to think about the jobs they can get with a college degree rather than about becoming educated so that they can begin to understand life and increasingly choose how they most wish to earn a living. To underscore that, during an interview I once threw in a favorite quotation: "What shall it profit a man, if he shall gain the whole world, and lose his own soul?" My interviewer on that occasion had recently had the benefit of a modern professional education. "Oooh!" she exclaimed, "I do like that! Who said it?"

Note

1. David Riesman with Nathan Glazer and Reuel Denney, *The Lonely Crowd: A Study of the Changing American Character,* New Haven & London: Yale University Press, 1950.

2. In newer subdisciplines, however, even in the sciences, that is not always so: computer science is a contemporaneous instance, a field that doesn't know whether it is science or engineering (or how much of each), whether publication should be science-style in journals or engineering-style in conference proceedings. But so far as tenure is concerned, the question is purely academic—a computer scientist denied tenure can find another university position quite easily or can choose to settle for a much higher salary outside academe.

10

Toilet Training

"Women need mentors," she continued, "and they must have access to the unwritten rules, the tips and advice that men exchange as a matter of course in their private get-togethers, like in men's rooms. . . ."

There were gasps and jocular exclamations around the room, guffaws, and the comment, "Anyone who tries to talk business with me in the john gets a fist in the nose." Of course, the gathered deans and chairs were almost all males, so I suppose it is only natural that their responses were like my own (which I had learned to keep to myself).

This incessant talk about mentors struck me just as did the endless questioning on how to get tenure. How long ago is it, I wondered, since it was just assumed that one did one's job to the best of one's ability, and if that was good enough then one got a chance at a more responsible job? Surely it's still true. Do well enough as an assistant professor and you'll be promoted to associate with tenure; do well enough at that and you'll be promoted to full professor. Any full professor with a respectable record and passable personality can get to be a department chair; and that job done reasonably well makes one a prime candidate for dean or vice-president or even president. At every stage, one has ample opportunity to learn things relevant to the next job; and if one doesn't so learn, then it's not a good sign of one's aptitude for that job.

If one doesn't understand what it takes, one shouldn't get there. Under the American Dream, anyone can become president, but not everyone does. Should we set up a mentoring system so that everyone somehow gets an "equal" crack at it? Or is it perhaps better just as it is, where those most suited to the job at any given time emerge through many stages and facets of competition? Can we in fact know what we shall most need or want in a president, even a few years from now? Do we not in fact want presidents who surprise us a little, who *lead*, in other words? Are not Franklin Roosevelt and John Kennedy, for example, remembered most for what they brought personally and uniquely to the office, things that perhaps we didn't even know beforehand were needed? Is it not much the same with positions of responsibility in any field, that one doesn't want technocrats, trained by business administrators and teachers of teachers, but individuals of ability with the desire to *add* something to the way the job has previously been seen, the desire to *mold* the position so that things can go better than they ever did in the past?

In academe, devotion to one's discipline and devotion to the life of the intellect ought to be the touchstones for advancement, and no one learns those things through a couple of years of "mentoring." One doesn't need to have had much experience interviewing candidates to know what is generally sought in academic administrators: a record of successful teaching and scholarship, a reasonable variety of experience or some other sign of flexibility, understanding gained during those years by observing and by thinking, and a personality that promises fairness and integrity. Wanting an administrative job badly is usually the kiss of death as far as getting the job is concerned, and I fear that those who speak of the need for mentors usually do want quite badly whatever job they are after.

There is a sound basis for the prejudice that wanting the job too badly is the kiss of death: one doesn't want administrators who get their kicks out of *being* chair or dean or whatever; one wants those who get their kicks out of *doing* the job, and doing it in the manner that faculty would approve of. That is most likely to happen when professors get tired of the unsatisfactory administrators they have suffered and decide to do it themselves, properly. No one has mentored them, except in the trivial sense that we are all mentored by our experiences, if we have the wit to learn from them. Professors learn, usually through years of a certain amount of frustration, how universities ought *not* to be administered, and they can bring something new and valuable to the job by trying potentially better approaches that they have conceived for themselves. No advice, tips, or generalizations can substitute for the experience of countless illuminating, instructive incidents involving a variety of people, with subtleties and nuances that one can hardly instruct others about, and which are significant precisely because of their interplay with one's own sense of values and ideals about the academic enterprise.

One hears of the need for mentoring not only in relation to administrative positions, of course, but also for women who want to get a faculty position in the first place or who, having gotten one, want to get tenure or promotion. I've tried to recall what mentoring for that I might have had, and I couldn't. I learned from the people under whom I studied, but it was by observation and not from anything they said to me in the attempt to be instructive. Nor were they the "role models" that are talked of as frequently as are mentors. I studied with people whom I admired and respected and whose memory I cherish and often recall; but I had no particular wish to be exactly or even approximately like them, to emulate any of them in any particularities. They were quite human, and from each of them I learned—by observation and by thought—not only about strengths for the work at hand but also about the weaknesses and ineptitudes and follies that beset even the nicest and most capable and successful people. I didn't want to be like any of those "role models"[1]—I wanted to be a *better* teacher and a

better researcher than even they were. What I learned from
them that was of most value to me, I believe, was the faith that
if one did one's present job well enough, then good things would
happen to one. I also learned from them contempt for academic
and other politicking, for attempts to finagle the outward appearances of success without the substance.

I certainly had no mentor who prepared me for an administrative position. Quite the contrary, I was trained to an ethos
in which administration is seen as an inferior pursuit to the
teaching and scholarship that it exists to support. My most cherished and devoted "mentors" could not understand it when I
took up deaning; they wished me well, of course, but it was clear
that they were aghast and hoped soon to see me recover my
senses.

I'm not entirely alone in believing that mentoring is what
learners do for themselves by observing and by thinking, not
what anyone else can do for someone who wants to learn. Among
the most surprising and cherished compliments I have ever received were a few from people I have liked and admired and
who thanked me for what they had learned from me about administration. Beyond any doubt, however, they learned whatever it was entirely by themselves. I've never had the presumption to attempt to give advice to others about such matters
(except, of course, when I'm occasionally asked to discuss some
specific and interesting or knotty problem; or when I write my
memoirs). I'm clear about a few of the things I wanted to do as
dean: to maintain a perspective appropriate to a member of the
faculty, to act out of principle and not expediency or for pop-
ularity's sake, to keep personal biases as much out of my decisions as possible, to put *doing* the job ahead of keeping the
job. But surely those are all obvious things, are they not? And
I'm much more aware of the times when I failed to behave like
that than I am of having exemplified those ideals. If others
learned from me any particularities about the "nuts and bolts"
of administration, I can't imagine what they might be. Those
who benefited from having me as a "mentor" did so because

they didn't need a mentor—they learned for themselves, in an environment that happened to include me.

I like to think of myself as an individual, identifiably different from others, including others who hold similar jobs; and if I can find satisfaction from things I've done, it is when I believe that there are things I've done that others might not have. Of course, I did acquire from outside of myself certain ideals against which to measure my performance, but I acquired those ideals *for myself* and not from conscious or deliberate instruction by others. I learned contempt for sham from some of my teachers, not because they preached that, but because they exemplified it; and I learned it probably less from any of my teachers than from the great people about whom I read and heard.

I like to think of women also as individuals, and I like to think of them as being as capable as anyone else of learning from everything to which they are exposed, through reading as well as through living. I like to think that women are as capable as men of devotion to intellectual activity and what that entails— all things to which gender is entirely irrelevant. Those things to which gender *is* relevant are also peripheral to the academic life and must be resolved by each individual woman for herself, just as they must be resolved by each individual man for himself: to marry or not; to have children or not, and if so, when; how to organize housework, vacations, social life, and so forth. One who can be a first-rate philosopher, say, can surely take those sorts of issues in stride. Quite a valid saying, I think, is, "If you want something to get done, ask a busy man to do it." That gender is irrelevant to that aphorism is illustrated by the finding[2] that in academe the married women with children are at least as productive as the childless married women or the unmarried women.

Women are individuals; and the qualities desired in academics and administrators are in any case so rare that it is individually striking qualities that count most, or should count most. There are many men, after all, about whom one might say, "If only they'd had the right mentor . . ."; but would it even or ever be true? Do we really want in responsible positions people who don't have what it takes to learn for themselves? Some of the worst administrators I've known suffered from insecurity and lack of self-confidence,[3] and thereby made countless others suffer mal-administration. If someone doesn't feel ready for a particular job, indeed, feels the need for a mentor, should that person ever be appointed to that job?

That's what I dislike most about this myth of mentoring, that it discounts what one can only do for oneself and what one ought to do for oneself. Making a career means making oneself capable of doing the jobs one aims to secure. Becoming so capable, like all learning, is the result of one's own activity and not of instruction by others; it is so with students in formal classes, and it is surely so in other matters of learning. Administrators can benefit from a host of things: from understanding what moves people, from knowing what has been thought about education, from knowing themselves, from having information about the widest range of topics and disciplines . . . there can hardly be a piece of knowledge, or an insight, or a person encountered, or an event experienced that cannot be drawn on for useful help when one tries to do an administrative job. No mentor can substitute for such years of active learning. Perhaps a mentor can give a finishing gloss of some sort, but not to a product that doesn't yet exist. Sadly, the talk of mentoring seems to come mainly from or about those who have hardly yet got their feet wet.

*   *   *   *   *

"Isn't it wonderful," she said to me, "that there are conferences like this to help people get ready from the very beginning for an administrative career?"

For once, I was absolutely and uncompromisingly untruthful: "Yes," I said, "it is."

I was newly a dean, at a workshop for new deans; and there was being held at the same time and place a conference for "future administrators"; and some of the sessions were jointly for participants in both conferences. She was an assistant to the dean, three years out of graduate school and two years into a faculty position. She had no particular interest in teaching or in doing research; she wanted to administer people who were doing those things. I thought it would be extraordinary if she could ever learn, from the outside so to speak, what universities ought to be about. I doubt that she—or anyone else—could acquire a proper empathy with good professors without having been one herself, and I further believe that such empathy stands administrators in good stead. Things being as they are, however, she will undoubtedly get the jobs she think she wants, and perhaps she will do them not much more badly than some who have had a more appropriate preparation for them.

* * * * *

Becoming capable of doing a job is only one thing, of course; making others take note is another. But the two are closely linked, as they ought to be. Success in teaching and research, plus some common sense and interest in others, make one potentially a capable administrator; and success in research automatically brings one to the attention of others. Admittedly, mentors can be directly helpful here, but again only if you-the-product already exist. It can be helpful to be nominated for a position by well-known people, but not if you don't measure up to the terms of the nomination. If you do measure up, then you will in any case have met people who can make the desired nomination.

It is just the same with women as with men, it seems to me: the capable ones get on with the job and the others complain that they are being hindered or discriminated against, if only through not being helped with their "professional development." I think also that the women's movement is in some respects like the earlier student revolt against reality: a few articulate middle-class liberals, ideologically crippled, converted their individual frustrations into a bill of goods that academe bought for a while. But *individual* qualities and merit still count, and always will. (I'm broadminded enough to admit, however, that the disasters wrought have had some beneficial side effects:

the capable women, who never complained in the first place and who rarely joined the movement, are being recognized more readily nowadays.)

Mentors can't do all the things you hear they can do for you. Moreover, as Kenneth Mellanby has remarked, in retrospect we come to realize that our mentors had tongues of clay.

Notes

1. I always found it incongruous when lesbians on our faculty carried on about the need for more women faculty to serve as role models for the students.

2. Tessa Blackstone, "The Scarce Academics," *Times Higher Education Supplement*, 16 March 1973, p. 13; Jonathan R. Cole and Harriet Zuckerman, "Marriage, Motherhood and Research Performance in Science," *Scientific American*, February 1987, pp. 119–25.

3. They had not an inferiority complex but an inferiority simplex: they felt inferior to others and indeed they were.

11

Public Forum

One day, quite early in my tenure as dean, my secretary came into the room: "There's a student on the phone, and I checked, she really does need to talk to you personally for a minute. She's secretary of some student group, I didn't catch the name, and they want to put on a public forum and called to ask whether you'd be willing to be moderator for them."

Clearly this was something a dean ought to be ready to do. I picked up the receiver and said: "Hello, yes, my secretary told me what it's about. I'll be happy to do it as long as the time you're planning on is possible for me."

"Oh, wonderful, thank you," I heard. "We thought we'd give you plenty of notice, it's still some time away, and we want to set the actual date so that it will definitely be convenient for you." So we settled on a specific date and arranged that she would drop by the office soon to give me further details.

A few days later, Irene came to see me. She was secretary of the Gay Students Alliance, and they were planning a Gay Awareness Festival; the public forum was to be a panel of several homosexuals, male and female, some of whom had not previously "come out of the closet" and who would explain and discuss the subtle as well as overt discrimination to which gays were exposed. There would be comments and questions from the audience, and so they had particularly wanted someone with official standing, like the dean, to be moderator in case any rowdies showed up.

"And of course," she assured me, "when I introduce the panel and you, I'll make clear that you yourself are not gay."

After she left, I made myself a promise that in future I would get all details about whatever I was being asked to do *before* agreeing to do it.

*   *   *   *   *

I have rather old-fashioned views: I regard homosexuality as an aberration or illness, not as an "equally valid life-style" or whatever the current euphemism may be. As with many aberrations and illnesses, I do not necessarily hold the individual responsible for being ill, and I do not believe that illness is criminal. Again as with many illnesses, I believe that some mixture of genetic or hereditary predisposition combines with environmental exposure to produce the actual condition: I suspect that some people are fated essentially from birth (or even before) to have homosexual inclinations, that others are molded strongly in that direction through early up-bringing, and that some others practice homosexuality almost purely as a matter of choice (in prison or in the armed services, for example). I also believe that life offers to homosexuals certain difficulties in addition to those life offers the rest of us, and therefore—if for no other reason—any given individual is better off being heterosexual than homosexual; I believe, too, that anyone who has a choice in the matter had better opt for heterosexuality. I worry that the opposite choice may be made by a larger number than otherwise, if they are exposed at a crucial time or age to articulate, well-meaning, nice gays who push the view that theirs is a completely viable and legitimate and truly "alternative" life-style. Thus I am not entirely in sympathy with gay student alliances, gay awareness festivals, or public forums to explain the validity of the gay life-style. I don't approve of proselytizing by gays; and I think it's very difficult to draw a line between free speech about civil rights for gays and the tendency for the life-style to be presented as something that it would be perfectly all right for anyone to choose.

But those sentiments belong to me as an individual, not to me in the role of dean. I-the-dean ought to treat in the same way all official student organizations, not influenced by the prejudices that I-the-man happen to possess. Just as my personally jaundiced view of fraternities gives me no right to discriminate against them through official decanal action, so too, if the dean is prepared to be moderator for a student group, the dean must be ready to be moderator for any and all student groups. Actually, even had I known beforehand precisely what occasion I was being asked to attend, I would have agreed.

* * * * *

At the panel discussion, Irene gave a good introduction. She told the audience that the GSA had planned the forum to show the public that gays were just like other people: the stereotypes of effeminate men and masculine women were quite misleading, applicable if at all to only a very small sample; most homosexuals could not be identified through their appearance or public behavior. And then, good to her word, Irene said that she had promised to make clear that I was serving as moderator only on account of my decanal position, and that I was not myself a homosexual.

In my subsequent brief remarks I commented that prejudice against gays ran deeper than perhaps even Irene herself realized; that despite their protestations, gays themselves do give some credence to the common stereotypes.

"For instance, Irene has just told you that no one, including gays themselves, can by appearance or public behavior identify another person as gay. And Irene was also good enough to tell you that I am not myself homosexual. How, I wonder, can she know?"

It was one of my better lines, and produced a gratifying response. When the applause had died down, I risked another punch line: "And, no, I'm not going to tell you."

* * * * *

I've said that I-the-dean really had no option but to accept the invitation to moderate that panel. Would I-the-man have accepted such an invitation? I'm not all that sure that I know myself, but in any case I'm not going to tell you. The point of this story is intended to be not only that personal biases should not influence official actions, but also that I-the-dean could not afford to reveal what prejudices I-the-man happened to possess—for no one would then believe that I could control them in my official activities. So as dean I found myself able to confide least in others precisely on those occasions when I most wanted to get personal counsel, to talk things through with some disinterested human being.

A dean qua dean has no friends, and a dean qua dean encounters no disinterested people. A dean cannot be a personal friend to any of the department chairs, lest the others suspect favoritism toward that department. A dean cannot, of course, practice personal friendship with any members of the faculty, because that would make the chairs of those departments nervous. A dean cannot fully confide in the vice-president lest the latter second-guess the dean's judgments. And a dean cannot confide fully in the deans of the other colleges in the same university, since they must always be in some part competitors for budget, space, and other things. So it is indeed a lonely job, lonelier in practice than I had anticipated even though these generalities had been fairly clear to me from the outset. And I think now that it must also be a much more difficult job for someone who is other-directed than for someone who was educated to be tradition-directed or inner-directed.

At any rate, I knew that I had to practice self-restraint with my purely personal opinions, especially about the touchier subjects. For example, our various women's groups knew I was a male and therefore knew already, without any help from me, that I was prejudiced against their cause and against their specific cases. I didn't need to exacerbate matters by, for instance, flaunting one of my favorite quotes, from the late senator Sam Ervin regarding the Equal Rights Amendment: one should vote for the latter, Ervin once said, only if one believed that God made a mistake in that he created two sexes.[1]

Even when I thought I was positively helping the women's causes I found my actions liable to be misunderstood. Typically the groups on our campus were founded by the younger and more radical women: instructors and graduate students and untenured assistant professors were much more active than the tenured and senior women. In consequence, some of the calls for action tended to the naively extreme, as for instance the publicly offered suggestion that half the deans be asked to resign within the next few years so that women could be appointed in their stead.

It seemed to me that such ill-considered proposals publicly made by groups professing to speak for all the women on the staff and faculty could only damage the actual women's cause. So I took to suggesting, to some of our senior women when I encountered them, that perhaps if they took a more active part in these organizations it would be of benefit all around. After some time, one of them told me that the game was up: word had gotten around that the dean was trying to get his cronies to infiltrate the women's groups.

Note

1. What would Ervin have said, I can only wonder, about the feminists who claim that "the rules of the academic game have been defined by men, and . . . women therefore feel profoundly outside (and *we are not using the terms 'women' and 'men' as biological categories, but assume that we all agree that these are primarily social constructs)*" (emphasis added) (Steven Rose, ed., *Towards a Liberatory Biology*, London: Allison and Busby, 1982, p. 15; quoted in Gisela T. Kaplan, "Coming Up with Bright Ideas: Women in Academia," *Vestes (The Australian Universities' Review)*, 28, no. 2 [1985]: 19–22). Such notions are also discussed, for example, in reviews by Alison M. Jaggar and Carol Sternhell, *New York Times Book Review*, 3 May 1987, p. 3. To be honest, though, I must admit that my friends and I had harbored

similar sentiments when we first started our careers in academe: we thought it was run by a bunch of old women, and quite obviously we were using that term as a social construct and not as a biological category.

12

Conflicts of Interest

"Professor Brien continues to perform superbly in all ways," it was my pleasure to read. "Her research is extremely productive and is attracting favorable national attention. She is equally effective in the classroom, and her service to the department sets high standards of enthusiastic professionalism."

I was perusing the faculty evaluations that our chairs sent me each year, and I had come to one of the most enthusiastic. Professor Brien had been just as outspoken in her praise of her chair (all faculty were periodically invited to tell me of their satisfaction or otherwise with the departmental leadership): "Professor Derek is an outstanding chairman. His scholarly productivity sets a marvelous example for all of us, yet he is also unstinting in his devotion to the department's collective welfare. He is fair and supportive." And so on.

This was all very gratifying, of course, but it struck me as a little odd, a little disingenuous—for in private life Professors Brien and Derek were wife and husband. How, I wondered, could they imagine that they were equipped to render impartial judgments on each other?

There were other couples, I hasten to add, who handled with much more insight and sophistication the separation that would seem to be called for when two people who are emotionally committed to one another interact also in professional activities. On occasion, people who were simply personal and platonic friends had asked to be relieved of assignments that would have required them to make judgments about one another, for tenure or in disputes between a professor and a student, for example. But in a few cases I was confronted with people who seemed not to understand the delicacy of these situations: first, no human being can be sure that personal feelings for a friend or lover will not get in the way of being impartial about that person's abilities and achievements; second, even if one is capable of exercising such superhuman objectivity, the rest of the community is not likely to believe it, and the *appearance* of impartial decision-making is quite as important as the fact that the decisions are reached impartially.

More and more frequently, we had to talk about these matters and related ones. We might want to hire someone who would not join us unless the spouse also found employment: would it be proper to pull some strings to make that happen? On the one hand, AA/EEO procedures made it mandatory to advertise openly every position: would it be in the proper spirit to draw up an advertisement uniquely shaped for the spouse of someone we wanted to hire? Would it be in the proper spirit when the spouse was a man, and this was the only way in which we could hire an able woman, particularly in a field where women are scarce? But if we did it in that case, could we refuse to do it when the spouse happened to be a woman? What if the couple were not married but were living together? If we did hire a couple in this way, what could or should we do if the couple separated after we had hired them? Would we begin to see marriages of convenience used not for the traditional purposes but to obtain academic positions? If we were agreed that we should do this sort of hiring, what if the couple were of the same biological sex?

Quite evidently, no written policies can be evolved to cover situations of this sort, if only because the relationship between two people cannot be guaranteed to remain the same over any period of time and because the closeness of such relationships ranges over a continuum and cannot be categorized into a few neat classes such as "married" and "not married." So everything depends ultimately on the sensitivity and sense of propriety of the individuals concerned. On a number of occasions I wished that everyone shared the understanding of how to keep personal and professional activities separate that was exemplified, for instance, by President Harry Truman: As the story goes, someone who was visiting Truman in the Oval Office was ushered in just as Truman was taking a postage stamp out of his wallet and affixing it to an envelope. The visitor expressed surprise, having believed that the White House enjoyed franking privileges. "Ah, yes," responded Truman, "but this is a letter to my daughter, and the franking privileges belong to the president of the United States."

* * * * *

Conflicts exist not only between personal and professional activities but between different sorts of professional responsibilities. The principle of academic freedom recognizes that the devotion and loyalty of academics go first to the search for truth and understanding in their subjects. If a conflict should arise between that and someone else's view of what the department or the university require, the rights of professors to follow their disciplinary conscience is safeguarded under the rubric of academic freedom. A professor's loyalty to department or university is somewhat conditional, therefore, and can be demanded only where there is no conflict between that loyalty and what the professor judges to be academically sound. To take a banal example, no matter how important to the university the president happens to think it is that some football player remain eligible to play, the president must not ask that a grade be recorded that does not properly reflect the athlete's academic performance.

Professors who take up administering also leave the arena in which one enjoys academic freedom. Every administrator must act within the bounds of institutional policy; and the chain of

administrative command also requires that administrators practice personal loyalty to those to whom they are accountable as
well as toward those who are accountable to them. A dean must
be loyal to the vice-president (and thereby to the president) and
also to the department chairs and associates and assistants and
other staff. If ever there is an irreconcilable conflict between
those loyalties, only one honorable option presents itself. Thus,
disloyalty may be proper grounds for removing an administrator,[1] whereas it is not proper grounds for removing a professor.

*   *   *   *   *

At times, there might seem to be conflicts between a professor's individual professional activities and the well-being of the
department. Thus it was quite fashionable, not so long ago when
grants were to be had for the asking (or were supposed to be
available for the asking), to deplore the behavior of academic
entrepreneurs who were said to be on campus barely long
enough to meet the occasional class in between their junkets
to Washington and their various conferences. How many living
examples of this could have been found, one does not of course
know; that there were ever whole departments composed of
such people, I seriously doubt. In the main, most every department should count itself fortunate to have a few such active
and distinguished people, and it ought to be happy to arrange
its work to reach a reasonable accommodation with them.

At any rate, the supposed disloyalty of such entrepreneurs to
department and to university used to be a standard source of
tut-tutting in departmental corridors and in the media. I am not
aware, however, that anything has been said about the deplor-
able situation that obtains when the very opposite is the case,
situations that do at times actually exist: departments whose
members are all so concerned (supposedly) with the welfare of
the department that they have no time or energy left to do any
individual work of their own. I came to regard it as a red flag
when a professor would say to me, "All I want is to do what's
good for the department. . . ." One or two departments seemed
to be in a constant state of revising their curriculum, changing

requirements for undergraduate and graduate degrees, altering committee responsibilities and composition, and the like, while scholarly activity was not much in evidence.

As in all things, the path of moderation would seem to be the soundest here. But if it had to come to a choice between two extremes, I would prefer a department of selfish entrepreneurs to one consisting entirely of self-proclaimedly selfless and public-spirited mediocrities.

Note

1. I recall an associate department chair, named Arrow, let us say, who disagreed with me about that. He and his boss, the chair, held opposite views about a number of things: how permissive to be with the office staff, how often faculty meetings should be held, what sub-specialties the department should emphasize. The chair was ready to fire Arrow because the latter was making his views public and was openly critizing those held by the chair. I talked with Arrow, pointing out the different role an administrator played than a professor, and I urged him to mend his ways or to resign. I was abashed, a week later, when I received a written response: Arrow thanked me for having made these complexities clear to him; "paradoxically," he went on, "it has made my resolve firmer to keep the position and to fight for what I believe to be right."

So he was fired.

13

"I Don't *Want* to Leave, But . . ."

"I really don't *want* to leave," he said, "but. . . ."

And I prepared myself to be insufferably bored. Not that this sort of conversation took place all that often, but when it did it was always so precisely the same. Most other occasions had at least slight individual variations, but these invitations to match offers from other universities were always the same: I heard the same non sequiturs, the same bluster and naively shameless display of vanity, and, beneath that, the same self-doubt.

We always talked past one another since we began with fundamentally opposite attitudes toward the situation. I had long tried to make plain, to faculty and to department chairs, that I disliked as well as disapproved of attempts to get more here by arranging for an offer from over there, and that I was not prepared to enter into such haggling. However, as with many other words from deans, these fell on deaf ears. The old myth dies hard, that the way to get ahead is to get offers and use them as bargaining chips. Social scientists in particular seem to accept this mythology as fact, perhaps because they regard everything as entirely political. Yet it was two of their number who exposed this particular myth long ago.[1]

In a sense, of course, it is true that one way to get ahead is to get offers; but only if getting ahead means to you little more than higher salaries, and if you are prepared to accept the offers as they come and to put up with the disruption of moving every few years, and if you don't mind the reputation you'll acquire, that of someone who tries to make everything count for a bit more than it's really worth, of someone whose work is of ephemeral rather than lasting value. If, however, you think that offers from other places can easily be cashed in for more dollars at home, you are likely to be disappointed.[2]

*   *   *   *   *

By the time this conversation would take place, Professor John Doe[3] had evolved such a fixed position that he could not give an inch on anything. He was so sure that he had only to bring me the offer in order to get it matched; indeed, he had already decided what he was going to do with those additional dollars, and in fact had likely made promises about that to his family. Too, he had long tried to convince himself that we had been short-changing him, as was now *proven* by the other offer, so that clearly he was *worth* what was being offered now from Someplace Else. Since he knew we were bound, by the rules of the game, to "match the offer," he also knew that he could choose to enjoy the higher salary without experiencing the costs of a move. When he then found that we would *not* match the offer, he was deeply shocked; and our failure to do so further hardened his belief that here he was simply not appreciated "at his market value."

In effect, it seems to me, the decision to leave had already been made, albeit implicitly and subconsciously only. Professor Doe had thought much about all the ways he was being shown and promised appreciation at Someplace Else, in contrast to being taken for granted and treated at less than true value here; and so he presented his demands in such truculent detail and so self-righteously that he could not back off if any of the demands were refused. More than one John Doe left, to my certain knowledge being sorry to leave but having no option, having painted himself into the proverbial corner.

And once again, it seems to me, other-directedness is close to the root of the matter. These bargaining professors appeared to be other-directed in the extreme: they displayed no other sense of what their work might be worth than the overtly expressed opinions of others; they seemed to have no other sense of their own worth than the opinions of others; and it made me no happier for or about them that they seemed so ready to have their worth measured in dollars per year. Despite their bluster, their projection of what some might take as inordinate self-confidence, they didn't *really* know whether they were all that good: their harping on numbers of publications, excellence of journals, invitations to lecture and to chair sessions—all that was as much to convince themselves as it was to convince me.[4] So when an offer actually came their way, it was *proof for themselves*, and served to make their attitude intransigent in the subsequent conversation. And here is also the root of the genuine desire not to have to accept the offer: the underlying fear that if they moved they would be expected to live up to a valuation of themselves which they suspected to exceed the reality.

This diagnosis fits with my notion that the degree of other-directedness tends to vary by discipline. Many more social scientists and somewhat more humanists behaved and sought to bargain thus than did artists, mathematicians, or scientists. And on the few occasions that some of the latter brought up the issue, it went rather differently. "Look," one of them said to me once, "I'd just like to talk with you, to help me think it through as much as anything, and perhaps to get your advice or guess about long-term prospects here. My work has gone very well lately, better than most of my colleagues or my chair seem to realize. Some friends of mine in other places have started to hint that they're going to try to get me there. But I'm happy here, I can do my work, I like the environment, my family likes the area. I just don't want to get into a situation where I can't explain to my wife why I refuse to move to a place with a higher reputation that also is offering a much higher salary."

Or, on a couple of occasions, we were alerted to impending offers not by the people concerned but by their colleagues. Such approaches I genuinely welcomed, because some of the best people do develop so rapidly that one can scarcely remain accurately aware of it: there can be a lag of years before a national reputation gained in some subspecialty by an assistant or young associate professor becomes common knowledge at home, particularly if the person is more concerned with the work than with blowing a trumpet about it. So these forewarnings were valuable, and several times we were able to bring our local valuation into line with the disciplinary one quickly enough.

But in the conversations with the blustering ones who brandished their offers as they entered the office, I hardly ever managed to reach any accommodation. With a wave of the hand they would dismiss all the significant advantages of staying, all the reasons that actually made them wish not to have to move: better library resources, perhaps, or better computing services, or advantageous arrangements about "overhead" on grants, or the high degree of flexibility we had achieved over years of effort regarding travel, leaves, teaching assignments—all the things that made it an attractive place to work and live were waved aside; that our fringe benefits were often more than competitive was also waved aside. Professor Doe regarded it as his right to have matched the salary dollars that were being offered at Someplace Else, to have his cake and to eat it too.

I used to point out that offers are never, as they put it, "at market value": offers are always significantly *above* "market value."[5] When Someplace Else wants a quantitatively oriented computer-using whiz who can also work in specialties A and B, it has no great number of possible candidates among whom to choose. If one of them is our John Doe, then Someplace Else will pull out all stops to get him: offer a big salary increase and whatever perks they can, considerably more than they do for John Dour who is just as good but who is already on the faculty at Someplace Else. (We, of course, do the same thing ourselves.) Naturally that creates an inequity so far as John Dour is concerned, but one handles that as one can, perhaps by giving Dour substantially larger raises than Doe for a few years once Doe is safely on board. All potential employers know that a move costs a person even more than expected beforehand, sometimes many thousands of dollars, at times an unfavorable change in mortgage rates, and as much as a year or two of disruption of one's research. Consequently, the offer has to outweigh those manifest disadvantages.

Sometimes I was able to get Professor Doe to recognize the *general* validity of these points, but he would never go so far as to apply those generalities to his own case; he still believed that we should "match the offer."

"If we matched the offer," I would say, "we would be creating here the same inequities that I've just been talking about, doing something extraordinary for you but not for the best of your other colleagues just because they happen not to have a current offer. Then they would see no other way to correct the inequities than to arrange for offers themselves and bring them to me for matching."

The typical reply to that, of course, would be, "Perhaps so, but that's your problem, not mine. Mine is to get paid what I'm worth."

Which was approximately where we had come in.

At times, Professor Doe could be more demonstrably irrational even than that: for instance, waving an offer from some "rapidly developing" Noplace Else that included a named chair and a halved teaching load to someone we had barely decided to tenure and might not tenure again, given the chance; from a "rapidly developing" Noplace Else that might, with great good luck, make it in a few decades into the league just below ours. Whereas on many other occasions Professor Doe could be very clear about the high status of our university, when it came to offers he could see only the dollar signs.

A few times I was even told that I should match, on an academic-year basis (that is, for nine months of service), what was being offered by Someplace Else for a calendar-year appointment (that is, for eleven months of service, the full year less a month's holiday). "But," I would point out, "you can make almost that much here right now, with summer salary from grants or teaching; and next year with only a normal raise you can make *more* than that here in that way."

Oh, but "it's *guaranteed* for me there. I don't really want to teach summers, and you know what's happened to federal grants, even the best people in our field can't always get summer support nowadays."

And I would think to myself, So much for how good you really are. Can you, I wonder, hear what you are saying? Aloud, however, I say, "What about your duties there during the summer? You wouldn't have it free as you do here, to choose for yourself each year whether to do research or to teach or just to recuperate and recharge."

But that hardly ever worked either.

Knowing how these conversations tended to go, a few times I tried a shortcut. After the standard opening, "I don't *want* to leave," I interrupted immediately: "I'm really glad to hear that, we don't want you to leave either, and I'm glad that you've realized the long-term advantages of not moving do outweigh these one-shot deals that other places tend to offer. Tell me, how are things going in other ways?"

But I never did get away with that; we always had to go through essentially the same boring rigmarole.

*   *   *   *   *

Professor Doe would, of course, complain about his salary or his raise even without having an offer to wave.[6] That salaries were public information, or at least could all be obtained if one tried hard enough, naturally helped enormously. The following is the unvarnished truth:

"Last year," Professor Doe said to me, "I was so pleased with my raise that I made a point of thanking the chairman; and you know I don't often do that." (No, indeed you don't, I thought, for this particular John Doe had a well-deserved reputation for curmudgeonly behavior.) "But now I've just seen what others got, and I'm madder than hell."

Not much that I'd be able to do here, I recognized, but temporizing never hurt, so I asked, "How did you happen to come across those comparisons?"

"Oh," he replied, "I found them in my mailbox. Someone had typed out a list of people and salaries and last year's raises, and I was near the bottom. Of course, not everyone was listed, it seemed like about half of the faculty only, but even if the other raises were all lower than mine, it would still only be average at best."

How charming! One of his public-spirited colleagues, I learned later, had prepared a carefully drawn list and had distributed it also selectively, with the predictable result and apparently sole purpose that a few individuals would feel denigrated. Unfortunately, we totally lack mechanisms or sanctions for dealing with people who do that sort of thing.

*   *   *   *   *

I'm so old-fashioned that some regard me as positively quaint where money is concerned. I feel good so long as my family doesn't want for necessities and a few comforts and seems reasonably content, and so long as that results from spending less than my income, even one penny less. I buy a new car (actually a new one for me, but used by others beforehand) when the old one begins to spend so much time in the repair shop that it gets frustrating. Every time I was reminded about my salary while I was still dean, I would feel embarrassed and guilty. I feel sorry for anyone who doesn't work in a university. And so on. Quaint, I admit: apparently the normal thing is to be other-directed, not to know you have blessings unless others point them out; not to know indeed whether you are well or badly off except by comparing yourself and what you have with others and what they have.

"Here I am," Associate Professor Turk Young would expostulate, "one of the most visible people in the department" (and not only in the way you mean it, would flit across my mind), "and I'm making thousands less than old Fuddy Duddy, who hasn't done anything for years and didn't do all that much then."

Turk Young might often be a humanist but he was rarely humane. Appreciation for old-timers I found to be sadly rare; few seemed to be aware (as I often made myself aware) that those old-timers had prepared the way for us. No matter how much "better" we might be now than they were then, we wouldn't be quite as good now if their efforts had not been as good as they were. The old-timers were now getting lower salary raises, they had heavier teaching loads, and they did much of the scut work for us. Did they have to be overtly denigrated too? Can boys really only come to feel like men by killing their fathers?

"You now make $2,500 less than Fuddy Duddy," I would say, after checking what the figures actually were. "That's not even a year's raise for you. He gets lower raises nowadays, so in just a few years you'll have caught up." (In salary, I would think to myself, not in maturity let alone in generosity.) "He's twenty-five years your senior, so that difference in your current salaries is like average raises of $100 per year separating you. Obviously that means that we are paying you very much more than we are him, *mutatis mutandis.*"

It was like water off a duck's back; the $2,500 now was all that counted.

"Well look," I would keep trying, "just when in your opinion should your salary have become equal to his? Obviously when you were first hired it had to be at a starting salary, and as you know our salaries have been quite competitive. And you have to admit that your annual raises have been substantial. Why even compare yourself to Fuddy Duddy? And if you do, surely you'll agree that decades of honest service to the university have to count for something."

Of course Young knew that, which didn't stop him from replying, "But we're a *research* university, aren't we?" And so on.

Other-directedness once again, it seems to me. It cannot be the actual monetary value of the salary differential that counts, for the Professors Doe and Young become outraged over differences of a few hundred dollars, over salaries that differ by a fraction of a single year's raise, and especially that some of their colleagues "clearly" get more than they "deserve." By how much is not the point, and sometimes it even seemed to me that a Turk Young would have been quite happy if I had somehow lowered Fuddy Duddy's salary rather than raising his own. What can that mean except that Doe and Young measure their own worth by how much they are paid? And, that being so, it becomes sadly clear that they could never be paid quite enough to make them feel properly secure and self-confident.

On a couple of occasions, though, Professor Doe would speak to me in absolute terms and not on the basis of comparisons with his colleagues. "I've got four children," he would say, "and I'll never be able to put them through college, I'll have to leave the profession if you can't help me."

Then I would show the flexibility that a dean must have, by invoking comparisons myself. "I do sympathize," I would assure Doe, "but actually your salary looks pretty good by national averages for your discipline and rank. Of course I agree that it ought to be different in academe, starting salaries have lagged miserably behind inflation; we've managed to stay competitive with other universities, but that's about it. I know it's less than would be desirable, but we're all in a market economy," and so on. Thus I tried to bring them gently to some semblance of facing reality; only rarely did I confront them with it bluntly—though I was sorely tempted when one Turk Young even showed me a detailed itemization of his monthly household budget. Intended to demonstrate that he really needed more, its effect on me was the opposite when I saw that his mortgage payments exceeded mine by a factor of two. He explained that he needed such a seemingly extravagant property because his children needed to have horses. Another large item in his budget was the monthly check to a former wife.

It was the dean's job, it seemed to me, to try to mollify the better faculty at least, to try to comfort and even inspire them when they felt down. It was not the dean's job to tell them that they were immature, irresponsible, and unrealistic, which was, however, what I thought on many such occasions. I had been brought up in the knowledge that debt meant ruin; it was a cast-iron rule to spend less than one's income. I have not outgrown that ingrained bias, and find that I cannot understand the Turk Youngs who bring children into the world without knowing how to support them, or who must have more expensive homes and cars than they can afford. And I grieve that life provides these examples of what I had thought far-fetched when I read Ayn Rand.[7]

*   *   *   *   *

After some experience of complaints about salaries and raises, I coined the saying, "Rewarding everything becomes rewarding nothing." But Professor Doe never appreciated it.

"Look," I would explain, "we *agree* that your scholarly productivity is just fine, and your reputation and visibility; that's why you got such a handsome raise."

Ah, handsome perhaps by some measures, but nonpublishing Peters had gotten nearly as big a raise as had publishing Doe.

"Well," I would counter, "he's been recognized for years, even outside the department, as a simply outstanding teacher, one of the best in the college or the whole university, and we surely all agree that teaching ought to be rewarded too."

Oh, of course, "but after all, this is supposed to be a *research* university. . . ."

If one measures one's raise only against everybody else's, it is all too easy to conclude that research or teaching or service is not adequately rewarded: whatever one's own best or favorite area of performance happens to be, it somehow turns out to be the one that is never adequately rewarded. If we measure ourselves against others, a merely "average" raise is taken as tantamount to an insult; anyone who doesn't get appreciably more than "average" clearly isn't very well thought of.

"Please don't think about it in that way," I would try; " 'average' is just a mathematical term, it is not a valuation of your performance. For every raise we award that is above the average, we have to give some that are below. Don't think of it as an 'average' raise but as the normal raise for people who are doing a truly commendable job."

Once I thought of a brilliant analogy: "Please don't confuse the dollar amounts with our actual appreciation of you and your efforts. It's sort of like with my daughter, who asked me, 'If you love me, why can't I have a car in college?' I explained to her that my love for her is unshakeable, but that it doesn't provide me the dollars to buy her a car and help her run it. So if you'll forgive the analogy, we do very sincerely appreciate your efforts, we're proud to have you on the faculty, but that doesn't mean that we have as much money to distribute in raises as we would really like to. The two things are determined by different factors, and we just never have enough money to do what we would really like with salaries."

Try it yourself and see whether it works better for you than it ever did for me.

*   *   *   *   *

Complaints about salaries and raises were usually argued on the basis that services rendered ought to be properly rewarded. Disagreeable as I found those conversations, unhappy as I was with the attitudes revealed, still I found it less distressing than the people who wanted to be rewarded *before* they had done something—an approach customarily expressed under the notion of "incentives." "If the university wants . . ." was the formula: if it wants me to publish, then it must give me a secretary and a research assistant and released time from teaching and perhaps a summer salary and travel money too; if it wants me to develop a new course. . . . Or there were generalizations: "The university offers its faculty no incentives to spend time advising students." And so on.

I never succumbed—until now—to the temptation to respond bluntly: "Do we have to provide 'incentives' also to professors so that they will grade honestly; or so that they will keep au courant with their subjects? Will professors only do their jobs if they are given identifiable and extra incentives or rewards for every aspect of their duties? How about some incentives from the university for deans to listen to wearisome, not to say unfounded, complaints?"

Notes

1. Theodore Caplow and Reece J. McGee, *The Academic Marketplace*, New York: Basic Books, 1958; Garden City, N.Y.: Anchor Books, 1965.

2. Particularly when the offer seems noteworthy only to the wishfully thinking recipient. One of our faculty, having been a tenured associate for as much as three years, felt amply ready to be promoted to full professor. To help persuade us, he put himself on the market and then came brandishing what he called "an impressive offer"—from a university inferior to ours, to become an untenured associate professor "with assurance of early consideration for tenure and promotion," but, as he emphasized, at a much increased salary (by a few thousand dollars). He expressed himself as incredulous when neither his chair nor I was suitably impressed. Another young associate wanted me to know how well known he had become nationally, having just been offered a position as an "advanced assistant professor." . . . One persistent complainer actually turned down an offer at a higher rank and at a much higher salary but then found it offensive when we drew the conclusion that he enjoyed clearly compensating conditions with us and didn't need an "equity" raise.

3. I never had a Jane Doe behave thus. Perhaps it is not too simplistic to see as typically macho the aggressive behavior of the offer-brandishers, and one can only hope that the assertiveness training being urged on women will stop short of advising them to behave similarly. As Dame Edith Evans once remarked, "When a woman behaves like a man, why doesn't she behave like a nice man?"

4. I am reminded of my perpetual surprise that candidates for all sorts of positions seem not to realize how disagreeable an impression they produce by offering lengthy annotations intended to demonstrate just how significant their credentials are and how well they fit the advertised position. Time and again, for positions ranging from chair to vice-president, I saw applications rejected on sight by the screening committees because the lengthy covering letters attempted to make

for us the judgment that could only be ours to make. An understated application is so much more enticing: a brief resume, with a few indications of high quality that no one could miss—for example, the listing of very prestigious people as references. For a senior faculty position, the most impressive application I ever saw did not even include a complete listing of the candidate's publications: instead, there was a nice little list of publications *by others* about the candidate's notable contributions to the discipline.

5. One Professor Doe began his conversation with me as though seeking advice: "What should one do if one's market value is ten or twenty thousand dollars higher than one's salary?" I fear the numbers had a different impact on me than he intended.

6. It is worth bearing in mind that complaints stem from the complainer's view of a situation: they do not necessarily—or even usually—indicate that anything needs fixing. Thus all psychologists know (in principle, though in practice they apply it as little as others) that some people see their cups to be half full whereas others see them to be half empty. The experts of administration have just rediscovered that scientifically: satisfaction or dissatisfaction has less to do with the work environment than with the personality of the worker. See "Research News—Personality Traits May Predict Worker's Job Satisfaction," *Chronicle of Higher Education,* 10 December 1986, p. 7.

7. Particularly *Atlas Shrugged* (New York: Random House, 1957) and the attempt to establish a utopia by providing each person with somebody's perceptions of that person's need, instead of paying people what they can earn as freely established through supply and demand. "From each according to his abilities, to each according to his needs," I had thought to be a long-discredited notion. But not for everyone, it seems. One of our distinguished professors once brought me, in genuine distress, a letter written to him by a young instructor in the same department. Had he thought, the letter asked, of giving some of his so-high salary to the younger people in the department who were raising children and couldn't make ends meet?

14

Democracy

"That," I used to hear quite often from one of my mentors, "is what puts the *mock* in *democracy*." He would be referring to imperfections associated with the workings of committees. Perhaps his favorite illustration of that was the following memorandum, which he had carefully preserved: "A special meeting of the faculty . . . will be held. . . . *Business:* Discussion of the First Report of the Committee appointed by the Faculty to Consider the Second Report of the Faculty's Committee on First Year Courses (enclosed)."

One notable but less humorous occasion had to do with a Ph.D. candidate. The setting was another country, where the custom was for the whole of the graduate faculty to deliberate over the award of the degree, basing its judgment on reports from three or more examiners who had read the dissertation. This candidate—let's call him Brake—was well past seventy years of age. A born gadgeteer and inventor, he had made a good career in medical technology and had also, in his spare time and as a hobby, developed a novel technique in analytical chemistry; he had published papers on that, and a book, and his work was quoted in articles and monographs and texts. But Brake had never had a university education, and after his retirement he decided to make up for that. So he set to work and was after a reasonable time awarded a bachelor's degree. Next he set his sights on a doctorate. He wrote a dissertation that was based on several papers he had earlier published about that analytical technique, and one of the examiners found two points of difficulty which he felt compelled to draw to the attention of the faculty: first, the work was not new, since Brake had published those articles a number of years ago; second, the dissertation was written in an old-fashioned style—in the first person rather than the third person, which had been customary in scientific articles and dissertations for several decades.

My mentor supported the award of the degree. Brake, he pointed out, already enjoyed an international reputation in the field and had done so for a long time; indeed, the calibre of his work exceeded that of many successful recent dissertations. The matter of written style was surely not important, as the work was described clearly and fully. Brake, he suggested, might well be regarded as similar to the famous Michael Faraday, who also had not been university-educated but whose name lives in the textbooks and in the designation of one of the units in which electrical charge is measured.

But Faraday, pointed out another member of the faculty, had never held a Ph.D., so why should one be awarded to Brake?

Perhaps, suggested my mentor, because it would honor our university to have Brake holding one of its degrees. We would be adding prestige as much to the degree as to Brake as recipient of it.

But the faculty could not bring itself to concur with the majority of the examiners and to make an exception in this veritably unique case, and so Brake was never awarded a doctorate.

*   *   *   *   *

The conventional wisdom already knows, of course, that committee deliberations are wearisome and that committee decisions can sometimes be painfully inappropriate—"a camel is a horse designed by a committee." That recognizes the compromising that takes place among the members of most committees, compromising not only along political lines but also among honestly differing ethical or intellectual viewpoints. Such compromises can produce results that make little sense.[1]

Because committees are never of one mind, they need clear guidelines if they are to function appropriately; and clear guidelines mean written guidelines; and so governance by committees, which academe seems to think desirable or necessary, breeds bureaucracy and inflexibility: committees have neither the experience nor the will that occasionally permits individual administrators to make appropriate exceptions to policies or procedures.

No matter how I tried, I could not always foresee the interpretations that might be placed on the written charges that I put to committees. I recall in particular one occasion on which my wording turned out to have been particularly inept and ambiguous.[2]

Dr. Spray had not been recommended for tenure, after a series of split votes and conflicting recommendations that led an appeals committee to suggest that an ad hoc committee be empaneled. I charged that committee as follows: "The decision not to offer tenure was crucially influenced by the belief that Dr. Spray's interactions with some students have been unprofessional; specifically, that he used in the classroom language ('four-letter words') deemed offensive by more than a negligible number of students. . . . The committee is asked to determine the accuracy of this belief . . . with a view to determining whether these charges constitute reasonable and accurate grounds for the decision not to recommend tenure." That, I thought, was a fairly clear charge: had Spray routinely used profanity, as alleged by some complaining students?

But the committee's findings made me realize that I had not expressed myself clearly enough: "Language that was both profane and vulgar was used in the classroom and was/is regarded by Dr. Spray as an integral part of his teaching style. . . . several students made negative comments about this. Most of those commenting negatively about his language went on to be quite positive about his teaching, however. . . . Although the lan-

guage may have been regrettable and unnecessary, only a negligible number of students indicated that they were deeply offended. . . . The committee wishes to express the difficulty it
has had in establishing a de facto code of conduct in the absence
of written guidelines. . . ."

*   *   *   *   *

Since that occasion, I have never been able to use the word
"negligible" with any degree of comfort. Part of my mistake
had been to assume that the committee and I shared certain
unspoken, axiomatic presumptions: that it is unacceptable for
a professor gratuitously to offend even a single student; that the
use of profanity in the classroom is not necessary for good teaching and is therefore gratuitous. But it is with committees just
as it is with computers: "garbage in, garbage out." If the instructions are not unmistakably clear—if the literal meaning is
not the same as the intended meaning—then a computer or a
committee will deliver an answer to the literal question, not to
the substantively meaningful one.

Not only the charge to a committee can influence or determine the outcome, the very act of establishing a committee can
produce predictable consequences. For instance, no committee
will find that it serves no function and should therefore be dis-
established. Thus, setting up a committee on affirmative action
ensures that, at least once a year, there will be broadcast pious
platitudes that we are not doing enough—entirely irrespective
of what may actually have been done (let alone what may be
conceivably possible). Further, the news that a particular committee has been established encourages people to discover work
for it to do: the establishing of a grievance committee, for example, ensures not only that grievances will be lodged but, more
fundamentally, that grievances will be felt. And, all too often,
a committee will deliver judgments that flow predictably from
its composition: if a grievance committee is composed solely of
professors, for instance, then it will almost invariably find that
malfeasance stems from administrators.

One of my sadder discoveries as dean was the degree to which administrators are not seen to be human. For instance, I found that our standing University Grievance Committee understood very well that anxieties beset professors but understood not at all that administrators too have their anxieties. Several of my department chairs had complained to me that they were summoned to appear before the committee without being told what it was all about, not even the name of the individual who had lodged a complaint; and naturally they had butterflies in the stomach during the days or weeks before the meeting eventuated. I met with the committee members and pointed this out to them; and I told them how careful I myself tried to be, to let anyone with whom I arranged to meet know exactly what the meeting was to be about.[3] The committee members were quite amazed: they were accustomed to seeing themselves as powerless because they had purely an advisory role, and they saw department chairs and deans by contrast as powerful. It was revolutionary for them to contemplate this alleged reality that the chairs and deans felt themselves threatened by the committee which was able, through its "advice," to make big trouble for them.

That grievance committee more than any other, perhaps, taught me that a committee has no memory. After I had talked with its members on that occasion, the committee was scrupulous to let administrators know why they were to appear before it—until the next academic year began and the committee acquired a new chair who had to learn the job from scratch.

Perhaps because that committee saw professors as powerless and administrators as powerful, it was very protective of professors and quite unprotective of administrators. Thus a professor could lodge a complaint, make allegations and—presumably—offer supporting evidence, all in total confidence. To protect that confidentiality, when we administrators were called on to respond, we were often not told what evidence had been proffered—we were expected to respond to the charge as though it had been established. We were, in other words, guilty until proven innocent. Now if that were to happen to a professor or a student or an outsider, most academics would quickly draw the analogy of McCarthyism or the Star Chamber; but where administrators are concerned it is different. Administrators tend to be seen more as cogs of the machine than as individual human beings, by committees even more so than by individual members of the faculty.

For me, the epitome of frustration was reached when I was found by the University Grievance Committee to have been guilty of some sort of bias, without that committee even having talked with me about the matter. Was it entirely inconceivable to them that I might have another side of the story; that whatever "facts" they had been given might support some alternative explanation? Ah, Rashomon. . . .

What recourse did I have, I asked our university attorney, when a committee put into writing words that impugned my integrity? None, was the answer; these committees are only advisory and their recommendations are legally protected. But even if I haven't been publicly libeled, I pointed out, I've been painted a villain and the portrait has been delivered to my immediate boss. Can't I even insist that I be given a chance to know what the charges are based on and what supposed supporting evidence there is? No, I can't, it seems.

Ah, well. Failing any way of obtaining substantive redress, one has no option but to take a wider perspective on these matters. As one of my colleagues used to put it, being a dean means being criticized, because no matter what goes wrong, there is always someone who knew it would; and if you ever find everyone going your way, then you may be sure that you're in the wrong lane.

As for the faculty, let the dean remember that those who are most moral are farthest from the problem. And committees are usually very moral, being composed of the most upstanding as well as the most outstanding professors. Inevitably they find it very hard to believe that any professor could possibly do what administrators occasionally charge a professor with doing (or with not doing). And so committees can become part of the problem.

Academics do well always to recall that virtue has to be its own reward. Deans, however, need to be aware that, for them, virtue can be its own punishment.

Notes

1. Thus one of our departments was resolved to elect its chair in the fairest possible way, through recognizing that each member of the faculty might have not only a favorite candidate but also favored second or third alternates. Every professor would cast votes for three people, in ranked order of preference. All first-ranked votes would be given a weighting of "3," second-ranked votes a weighting of "2," and third-ranked votes a weighting of "1." The candidate with the highest score would be declared elected, provided he had also attained a majority of the total possible score. Shortly after that procedure had been agreed to, the following memorandum was circulated by one of the more mathematically minded professors: "Suppose there are n nominees on the mth runoff election. If k professors each cast a ballot with 1st, 2nd, and 3rd choices indicated, then by the weighting scale currently adopted, the maximum score achievable by any one candidate is $3k$. However, the total score received by all candidates will be $(3k + 2k + k) = 6k$. Therefore, no majority will ever be possible."

2. I do not claim, however, to have achieved the standard set by the administrator who clarified the university's rules for renting automobiles. His memorandum read, in part: "Rental cars are to be used only after reaching the destination of travel, not for the means of travel to the destination."

3. Inadvertently I caused a few people much anxiety by forgetting to let them know what the topic of discussion was going to be. That made me realize that a dean could, failing the availability of other sanctions, enact punishment or retribution in the form of stress. The dean's secretary sets up a meeting with the intended victim, a couple of weeks in the future (everyone knows how busy a dean is), without

disclosing what the subject is to be. Just before the scheduled date, the secretary arranges a postponement; and that is repeated several times. Finally, the meeting is canceled without explanation.

15

Evaluations

"Don't you trust me?" he had asked, and I had thought to myself, Do we all become blithering idiots as soon as we become administrators? Or do we just learn that nobody should trust us anymore?

He, Hollins, had just become chair of the department in which I was a professor, long before I too became an administrator. Some of us had been exercised about the recently introduced evaluation of teachers by students: we were all rated, on a scale of 1 to 6, by all students in all classes; and of course the students were allowed to do that anonymously. Then a departmental ranking of ability in instruction was drawn up. My ranking on the first occasion was 12th out of 30, based on a score of 5.17 out of 6; and I had swung among incredulity, amusement, and outrage when I discovered that my colleague with a score of 5.18 was rated 11th, that 5.20 made two of my friends equal 9th, and so on.

It should be obvious that those scores are not sufficiently different as to warrant the ascription of different ranks. Indeed, some serious social-scientific studies have shown by proper methodology that even much larger differences do not provide a valid basis for comparing teachers; under some circumstances, at least, a teacher's score is much more significantly influenced by factors over which he has no control: the level of the class (freshman, upper-level, graduate), the size of the class, the hour of the day at which the class meets, whether the course is required or chosen as an elective, what grade each student in the class expects to receive. In fact, in studies where corrections were applied for these factors,[1] there remained relatively little variation among the scores of different instructors—which one might also regard as fairly obviously to be expected, given that rotten instructors are not appointed in the first place and don't remain long if they have been, and that a "good" teacher for one student may not seem so good to another.

At any rate, we were appalled to find ourselves ranked by instructional ability on the basis of doubtfully valid and insignificantly different scores. The only way, it seemed to me, to avoid significance being ascribed to such differences as between 5.18 and 5.20 was simply not to record or report numbers in that fashion: let the computer be programmed to calculate the scores to only two significant figures, so that in this case 5.2 and 5.2 would be all that anyone knew. (I was resigned to the fact that such differences as between 5.2 and 5.3, though clearly insignificant also, would be taken as significant; even as a professor I had been prepared to make some compromises with reality and to accept partial improvements with gratitude.)

And so Hollins had been moved to ask, "Don't you trust me?"

He didn't seem to understand that I trusted him fine, and as appropriate, but that I couldn't trust any human being, myself included, not to notice that 5.18 and 5.20 are different numbers. I had been taught that one should round numbers off so that only the significant digits are shared with others; that's what "significant figures" means. That one can generate numbers that look more precise is quite beside the point: "actually" my rating had not been 5.17 but 5.1749, and my colleague's had been not 5.18 but 5.1751; if the computer could be told to eschew meaningless third and fourth decimal places, could it not be told to eschew the equally meaningless second?

Hollins was far gone, however. He understood all that, he assured me, and he himself would never discriminate on such meaningless grounds. But he had to deal also with others, and if he wanted, say, to make the best possible case for someone for a raise or a promotion, it might be helpful if he could show the dean that Blank was not a mere 5.7 teacher but really a 5.74 one.

I knew when I was licked and gave up, having learned, however, that some chairs think that they can snow their dean with meaningless numbers, a piece of information that had some direct utility for me later; and that some chairs will try to conceal their own failings from their faculty by placing blame on the dean.

I'm also proud that after about five years of unceasing effort and pleading as dean, I was instrumental in causing student evaluations to be rounded off by the computer to only two significant figures—which may quite possibly turn out to have been one of my most significant and lasting achievements as dean; one, however, that few will know about or appreciate properly. It reminds me of a friend who was briefly dean of a graduate school and who confessed once that his proudest achievement had been to have altered the form completed by all candidates for admission, by dropping from the old form the requests for information about the candidate's height and weight. I think that truly was significant, because some prospective students and their mentors would be less inclined thereafter to confuse my friend's university with Podunk U.

*   *   *   *   *

When thought is given to how evaluations of any sort ought to be handled, there is generally agreement in principle that one should first be clear about the purpose[2] of the evaluation and then gather only information that serves the purpose. But in practice such thought is rarely given, and most evaluations are miserably flawed in consequence. Not only are the scores from student evaluations reported with more digits than is warranted, but the students typically are asked questions that they have no qualifications to answer, for instance, "Instructor's knowledge of subject matter." Similarly, when chairs are evaluated, their faculty are often asked to comment about such matters as the handling of the budget, about which the faculty usually know nothing and understand less. Information in evaluations ought to be solicited only from those who have some reasonable source for that information and some reasonable grounds for holding an opinion. As soon as a question is put, even if there is a space for "Don't know" or the like, most respondents feel that they should give an answer if at all possible, and do so even on the basis of secondhand information or plain hearsay.

Evaluations can cause difficulties not only because the wrong information is obtained, or because significance is attached to comments or differences that are not significant, but also because some of those who have provided information for the evaluation tend to believe that they have some stake in the outcome of the evaluation and should be apprised of the details of that outcome. Thus students periodically ask that their ratings of instructors be made public, so that other students can know which classes to take and which to avoid; and faculty want to know, after commenting about their chairs, whether the chairs have been told to mend their ways. It is little realized that many factors are considered in most evaluations, and that there also exists a narrow range of possible actions after an evaluation. Where a chair is concerned, for example, there is not that much room to maneuver between reappointing and replacing. Many complaints or dissatisfactions arise essentially from differences over personal styles of interaction, and few of us can change such habits. Again, it is quite rare that there is anything approaching unanimity even on such questions as that of appointment or reappointment; and it is usually a good idea, if appointing or reappointing, to make the person chosen feel truly wanted, by soft-pedaling or eschewing suggestions that might sound like criticisms.

On occasion, I tried to reason with professors who had expressed some difference or other with their chair. One had once passed on to me the rumor of what would have been quite a serious infraction by his chair, and I looked into that very thoroughly indeed. Delighted with the outcome, I phoned my informant to assure him that there was no truth at all to the allegation. He responded, "Thank you for letting me know, but I prefer to believe the rumor."

*   *   *   *   *

We can all be remarkably insensitive in such matters: we easily act as though our chair or dean or vice-president or president has no anxieties or insecurities, never wonders whether he is doing a good job, needs no reassurances. A couple of our departments, for example, carried on their own annual evaluations of their chairs, separate from and in addition to the university-mandated ones, which were not quite so frequent. A departmental evaluation committee would solicit anonymous comments from all the faculty, compile them, and give copies of the compilations to the chair and to me—no effort being made to cull out possibly or obviously erroneous or invalid or venomous statements. I can still not understand why those faculties could not comprehend my pleas that they cease committing these enormities upon their chairs.[3] In one instance, the volume of strongly negative comments greatly exceeded that of the positive ones, and both the chair and I were at first quite concerned; yet from the last university-mandated review I knew that a very handsome majority of the faculty were very pleased with the chair. It turned out that the departmental committee had compiled the comments by category (professional development, budget, etc.) in a manner that could not reveal how many individuals had made particular sorts of comments—and in point of fact the mass of negatives had all come from only two or three people. Those who had praise to give had done so concisely; those who had criticisms had gone on at great length.

The very occasional praise I received from chairs or faculty meant a great deal to me, and it always reminded me to do likewise to my vice-president and president, who appreciated compliments as much as I did (while also believing that it *shouldn't* matter to them). But I know I did it too rarely, for I have the same human tendency as others: to assume that my superiors know that they are doing a fine job and that my complaints to and about them are only to the specific issues and not about their performance overall; to assume that they have no anxieties and never wonder—as I used to—whether or when they should resign to make way for someone who could do better.

*   *   *   *   *

Candidates for promotion or tenure are evaluated in part on the basis of opinions about their work from well-established people in the same discipline at other universities. I kept urging our chairs to make plain, when these opinions were solicited, that we wanted to hear only about the merits of the candidate's scholarly work—the overall assessment and the actual decision were ours to make and would be based on teaching and service as well as on scholarship. Nevertheless, a certain proportion of those who gave us their views could not resist going beyond what we asked, and they caused amusement if not actual difficulty at times when they wrote something like, "Blackston certainly deserves to be tenured at your institution." Did that mean (our nitpickers on the committees would ask) that Blackston *wouldn't* deserve tenure at *the reviewer's* university? Or did it mean that Blackston deserved the punishment of lifetime servitude with us? Or was this really supposed to be a thoroughgoingly positive recommendation?

I learned of many pitfalls in the interpreting as well as the soliciting of these "outside letters." Some departments occasionally asked the opinions of eminences in other lands, and thereby invited trouble when not all the members of the various committees were sufficiently sophisticated or cosmopolitan: to know, for instance, that from Cambridge, England, "His work is quite solid," means roughly the same as from Cambridge, Massachusetts, "His work sets the standards for which the rest of us aim."

One of the most interesting aspects of these letters was how their tone varied according to the discipline. I can best describe those differences by offering examples.

The Mathematical Sciences

"Gowland has done a respectable amount of work, some of which I had known about before your enquiry. . . .

"Paper 1 tackles a problem that is not negligible, and the paper is nicely done even though no particularly creative approach was called for. . . .

"Paper 5 is a little gem. The exposition is beautifully concise, the core of the proof is elegant, and the hints of extended applications are appropriate. . . .

"Gowland is one of a rather small group working in circularly discursive operators functioning ringwise in fractal dimensions, and he is recognized as a significant contributor. While he has not shown the brilliance of Daytoni or the massive technical skills of P. Q. D. Smith, he is at least the equal of Matilda Rowson, John Trybes, or Peter Dzugga, who have been tenured recently in very good places. . . ."

The Natural Sciences

"Cook has published at quite a reasonable rate, in decent places. He has helped make the application of partition theory to oblong kinetics useful for analytical purposes, and in showing that he has also published some straight analytical papers. While those might be regarded just as turning the crank, it has actually been beneficial to demonstrate how well the theoretical possibilities work out in practice.

"The amount of grant support is OK for this field, but of course one would expect it to increase in the future. That he has already supported some graduate students is gratifying.

"I know from chats at Gordon Conferences that he is generally thought of as a potential leader, and I don't believe you can go wrong by tenuring him."

The Arts

(Typed or handwritten on paper that has no letterhead)

Dear Professor Brown:

I'm glad to hear you are considering Marrow for promotion to tenure. I've known him on and off for more than half a dozen years and am always glad to see him. He's a good fellow, a credit to the profession, and I'm happy to recommend him without reservations. Do remember me to him.

Sincerely,
[illegible]

The Humanities

"Charryn measures up about as well as one can expect to the unrealistic standards we seem to be setting nowadays. Your letter asks whether her work has shown signs of significance or distinction, which we really shouldn't expect to discern until someone has been in the profession for a couple of decades. . . .

"There is real promise in the edited material, signs of meticulous regard for the original documents yet a willingness to make the judgments that are the possible source of genuine distinction in such endeavors. . . .

"Of course you will be more interested in the articles devoted to literary criticism. . . .

". . . sometimes picayune, or far-fetched. . . . but what can one find new on this well-covered ground. . . .

". . . occasional insight that struck me as promising. . . . not yet as wise as she appears to believe. . . .

". . . quite well written, though . . . some signs of the unseemly haste that our present-day rush to judgment fosters. . . . a decent copy-editor (are there any left?) could probably. . . .

"I trust your University is not unduly tardy about paying the honorarium for these evaluations. . . ."

The Social Sciences

"Brown has published 15 articles, 3 of them sole authored, 8 with one coauthor who is not always the same person and 4 with multiple coauthorship.

"It is good to see some sole authored pieces to show that Brown is able to set up her own hypotheses, establish protocols for testing them, and bringing the results to publication. Moreover, these are in pretty good places with rejection rates of around 80%. Of course, she has yet to crack the very topflite outlets, like *Journal of Distinguished Interdisciplinary and International Social Science,* whose rejection rate is now at 98%, but that can come, and anyway not everyone has to get something published there, even some of their own reviewers never make it.

"It is good to see co-authored papers showing that Brown can get on with her colleagues professionally and combine her expertise with theirs. The indications are that her contributions to the work were significant, since her name comes first on about a third or a fourth of the coauthored articles. The journals here are perhaps a little better than with the sole authored pieces, the rejection rates are about 85%; but I'm not always sure that we ought to pay as much attention as we do to those numbers. . . .

"It is good to see that Brown has taught . . . different courses . . . student evaluations . . . graduate-level. . . .

"It is good to see . . . invitations . . . chairing sessions . . . officer. . . .

"It is good to see . . . departmental committees . . . university service. . . .

"I hope this is the assessment you were asking for. . . ."

Notes

1. Richard D. Shingles, "Faculty Ratings: Procedures for Interpreting Student Evaluations," *American Educational Research Journal*, 14 (Fall 1977), 459–70; Philip C. Abrami, Les Leventhal, and Raymond P. Perry, "Educational Seduction," *Review of Educational Research*, 52 (Fall 1982), 446–64.

2. In a department that was not, I'm happy to say, in my college there occurred the following. Professor Roe, who had served as chair for half-a-dozen years, gave a year's notice of his intention to step down, and during that year a national search was conducted to find a successor. In the event, none of the candidates was particularly attractive, Roe was offered tangible incentives to reconsider his decision to resign, and eventually he accepted the offer of another term in office. Now because Roe had given notice that he was resigning, there had not been conducted the regular triennial evaluation of the chair that would have been due during the year the search was conducted. But because Roe had now been reappointed, that logic was no longer persuasive. Therefore, a few weeks after Roe had been offered and had accepted a new term of office as chair—but before that term had even started—a committee began the work of evaluating his performance as chair.

3. One of the guilty professors (of not too mature an age) expostulated, "Oh, our chairman's tough—it wouldn't faze him, he takes criticism well"; whereas I knew that the chairman had hardly slept for two nights, wondering whether he should or needed to resign.

16

Tribal Stereotypes

What I enjoyed perhaps most as dean was the opportunity to come to know people from many disciplines and to learn something about their subjects. I came to discern what seemed to me characteristic attitudes particular to different disciplines—illustrated, for instance, by the letters of evaluation at the end of the previous chapter—and so I was led also to recognize the extent to which some of my own views had been shaped by the discipline to which I was trained. I like to think that this recognition helped me to ameliorate some of my biases and to become somewhat less dogmatic about certain preconceptions, and I offer that as justification for setting down here some stereotypes of practitioners of the various disciplines. If the grains of truth in these stereotypes do arise from the disciplinary training to which we are all exposed, it is as well to be aware of that; then, if we choose, we may be able to do something about it, individually or collectively.

*   *   *   *   *

The oft-cited dichotomy of humanists and scientists has some truth to it, though nowhere near as much as is thought by those who discuss it. Its greatest merit may be that it ignores altogether the so-called social sciences. At any rate, a dean soon learns that the academic tribes[1] are much smaller and more numerous than the asserted dichotomy of humanists and scientists implies: while all academics have a few traits in common,[2] and scientist-academics share some that humanist-academics do not, so also are chemists distinguishable from, for example, geologists; and there are differences to be found between physicists who are theoreticians and those who are experimentalists; and so on. So far as I am aware, the only serious attempt to study such differences was made by Anne Roe.[3]

The Arts

In some respects, the painters and sculptors and musicians and theater folk fit best my old-fashioned ideal of the academic: they were captivated by their art long ago, and it is their very life and not just a means to earn a living. They are almost unique in academe because they would earn even *less* money in a non-academic job. And they are entirely unique in thinking that teaching loads of about twenty contact hours per week are eminently reasonable since that leaves them some time for their own individual artistic endeavors and even for their families. Yes, families: the days are long past when the artists led unstable personal lives; the rest of us have caught up with and surpassed them in what used to be regarded as peccadilloes, and artists now express their unconventionality by leading family lives of some stability.

Given all those virtues, the more exasperating characteristics of the artists should be readily tolerable by a dean. The artists share with the humanists a high degree of innumeracy[4] and an inordinate pride in being innumerate. Their paperwork beggars description. And their emotions are charmingly spontaneous, with one another even more than with outsiders. Their chairs cannot grasp the point that salary raises and tenure and promotion ought not to hinge on how well the person happens to be liked by colleagues and by the chair. "What do you mean by 'objective evaluation'?" they would challenge me. As a minimum, I used to suggest, that a given individual could hardly be the most valuable member of the department in one year and the least desirable the next year. "Can't we correct our mistakes once we recognize them?" I would then be asked.

The artists are, on the whole, still a bit surprised to have been given a home in academe. The other academics regard the artists as not really genuine academics, at the same time as they enjoy and take for granted the visual, dramatic, and musical treats that the artists provide, usually free or at bargain-basement rates and without any special or extra recompense to the performers. In that sense all the artists are shamelessly exploited by the rest of the campus, but the degree of exploitation is unquestionably greatest of the musicians at the hands of the athletics department, which gets the benefit of a marching band for much less than its actual cost.

The many similarities among the musicians, theater folk, painters, and sculptors stem from the fact that their fields call for aesthetic sensibility rather than the intellectual approach that necessarily has primacy in the letters and sciences. Thus research or scholarship in the sense of articles or books hardly exists, is of no concern, is not particularly valued. The college and university must learn how to assess the artists for tenure or promotion by recognizing the differences among shows (local or regional or national, juried, invitational, etc.) and the significance of works bought into collections, invitations to perform elsewhere, reviews of performances or shows, improvement shown by pupils in voice or on instruments, and so on. Notably, there is no dichotomy of "pure" and "applied" in these fields. (In music, "applied" means lessons, usually individually given, for vocal or instrumental performers; if anything it is regarded as more important than lectures.)

Two subtribes, however, are different in most of these respects: the musicologists and the art historians. Their style of work is very much that of the historical or philosophical or literary scholar. They do not always feel at home in departments of music or art respectively; and it is not uncommon to find separate departments of art and of art history.

The Mathematical Sciences

There is said to be some close kinship of mind-set between mathematicians and musicians. But the only sign of it that I ever saw was in the temperamental behavior of some mathematicians, notably perhaps some of the "purists."

The "pure-versus-applied" dichotomy, found also in the natural sciences, is perhaps most marked in mathematics, where one even hears occasionally about the desirability of separate departments for these different subtribes. The "applieds" are much like some physicists, computer scientists, or maverick first-rate engineers (as in departments of engineering science and the like). The "pures" I found as charming, lovable even, as I do most young children most of the time (and equally insufferable at other times). As with the artists, the work of the "pures" is also their life; however, through being in constant contact with the "applieds," they occasionally realize what salaries and perquisites are enjoyed by others, and then they have temper tantrums. But there is no real malice in them; their chief characteristic is to be captivated by the beauty and elegance that their endeavors occasionally achieve, and one must simply remember that they know absolutely nothing about anything other than mathematics, and could care even less. When they dress like students of the late 1960s, for instance, it is no sign of rebelliousness—they just haven't noticed that most people around them don't dress that way anymore.

The statisticians have their "pures" and "applieds" too, and the former don't give the latter due credit for their yeoman efforts to bring a little rigor to the stuff that the aggies, the psychologists, and many others do. More and more questions of deep concern cannot be assessed without statistical expertise: environmental effects, claimed parapsychological phenomena, risks from drugs and food additives, and so forth. Yet, I was surprised to discover, the statisticians are still grappling with quite fundamental issues; for example, they don't even agree over what "probability" really means. Unfortunately they have not developed much facility in public relations, in letting the rest of us know how exciting and significant are their "pure" endeavors, and so they have to support that habit by doing much applied stuff.

Almost all disciplines and many other groups produce surveys (usually annually) of academic salaries by rank; however, the statisticians appear to be alone in recognizing that average salaries and ranges of salaries listed only by rank can cover (up) a multitude of other factors. So the statisticians' groups provide eminently useful compilations that show also quartiles and correlations with age or years in the profession or time in rank.

The computer scientists don't know what they are: theorists or machine builders or what. They *do* know that they're in demand, and that computers will in the broadest sense absolutely revolutionize human existence, and that consequently computer literacy is much more important for everyone to possess than is ordinary literacy or ordinary numeracy. Unfortunately they do not themselves know what computer literacy actually is or how it might be brought about.

The computer scientists accept outrageously high salaries as a matter of course, and emphasize that their needs for capital equipment (to be updated at least annually) are at least as great as in the natural sciences. Unfortunately they do not recognize that the natural scientists meet those needs themselves with funds from extra-university sources.

Computer scientists who work in industry are totally incapable of writing a comprehensible manual or guide for all the people who should use their machines to derive from them all the potential benefits. Computer scientists in academe are no better at explaining their enterprise and its needs to the rest of us.

The Sciences

According to the scientists, all useful and reliable knowledge is scientific knowledge, and all scientific knowledge—which seems to be defined as the knowledge about anything at all that happens to be possessed by one who is a scientist—is true and useful; what is not scientific is by definition neither reliable nor useful. "Science," of course, here means *natural* science, *hard* science.

Scientists claim that they have fun doing science, but at the same time they insist that it is fundamentally a serious business; after all, there is nothing more ultimately serious than finding out exactly how and why everything ticks: the universe, living creatures, the whole caboodle. In fact, scientists find it a little difficult to understand what makes some people do other things than science and even be misled into imagining that those other things can be equally worth doing.

Scientists are clear that you must *do* science in order to understand it, that you cannot get an appreciation of science by learning *about* it: you have to have actually experienced doing research. So science courses without labs are said to make no sense; interdisciplinary introductions to physics with chemistry with biology with geology are scorned as inevitably too superficial to be worthwhile. History of science may be OK if taught by scientists, as a small part of regular science courses: it's nice for students to know that Lavoisier made chemistry scientific, for example, and it's certainly useful to be able to label organic reactions by the discoverer's name. Philosophy of science is bunk, because the philosophers don't really understand what science is, never actually having done any themselves.

Only scientists, it seems, truly understand what research involves. They find it ludicrous to be expected to do good research, to be competitive, if they have to teach as much as a course every term. It's quite different, they will explain to a dean, for people who can do their "research" just by sitting in libraries or collecting data by surveys; you've simply got to have done lab or field research yourself to appreciate what it takes.

Scientists never have time to leave their labs for such occasions as coffee, lunch, or getting together with their families. They go away only to scientific conferences, where they spend no time at all listening to talks, a certain amount of time lobbying people from NSF and other moneybags, and a great deal of time in topless bars and other tourist traps. In those places, one may overhear such snippets as the following, about humanists and other nonscientists:

"I teach after a history class, and you wouldn't believe it: there's never anything written on the chalkboard! The guy just talks or reads from a book, and usually he's sitting down, even."

"Our neighbor's a philosophy prof, and my wife tells me he's always at home, usually just sitting in the sun reading a book. . . . Call that 'work'!"

"We've got a dean who's from English, and you wouldn't believe the troubles we have. He says we *exploit* our graduate students because we put our names on 'their' publications!"

"At our place, the humanists keep wanting to tinker with the curriculum. They think all students ought to take a lot of upper-level courses. You know what we found out? Their upper-level classes don't have any prerequisites! Can you imagine? And it's the same in the so-called social sciences! And they want us to make the students write essays all the time. . . . when would we ever find time for research?"

*   *   *   *   *

But the sciences are not monolithic. The physicists know that their subject is the key to the universe and that all other pursuits than physics—particle or high-energy physics, that is—are thereby inferior. Not that they are arrogant about it exactly—their certainty goes much deeper than mere arrogance. It is simply the natural order of things, which makes it also natural and obvious that Washington—the Congress and the president—should call on the advice of physicists on all important issues. For those who have grappled with quarks and tachyons and relativity, it is quite easy to think through such less difficult matters as defense policy.

The other sciences can be quite useful, of course, since they are all ultimately the application of physics; and some people in other departments may be virtually honorary physicists, for instance, some applied mathematicians and some physical chemists. Physicists are typically people of cosmopolitan and deep culture, who find it easy to read novels and even poems (whereas the humanists are quite incapable of reading science); and physicists have a natural aptitude for philosophy, needing no special training to speak or write about it.

Though chemistry is not the most mathematical of the sciences, in matters apart from the subject itself the chemists are the most quantitatively oriented of the scientists. They have a correct numerical answer to everything: how many graduate students there should be per faculty member, how many post-docs, how many papers everyone should publish per year. Whereas many other scientists have to travel to do their work— to national labs, geological formations, radio-telescopes, and so on—almost all chemists can do their work in their home labs. This makes possible a ready means of measuring the quality of a chemistry department: one counts how many people are in their labs on weekends and on such "holidays" as Thanksgiving or Christmas, and the highest count wins. An even easier measure, which doesn't require that one wander through the building, is to drive past at night and count the number of windows that are lit up.

The chemists are indefatigable about comparing themselves with other chemistry departments, through rankings of national visibility and the like. They publish compendia listing faculty members and their publications (research articles only are included, not books and especially not textbooks), so that the quality of the departments can be compared easily by counting column-inches. They send one another lists of their faculty and ask for help in assessing their national visibility: Are each of these people (a) known to you because of their national reputation; (b) known to you from reading their papers; (c) known to you from meeting them at conferences or hearing others speak about them; (d) known to you as authors of textbooks or innovators in pedagogy (that is, would they at least be useful as a director of freshman chemistry)?

All academics have the potential for being insatiable, and the insatiability of the scientists is by far the most expensive (leaving aside the computer scientists, who are in a class of their own; and the artists, who are phenomenally expensive per student or per faculty member but not in total because there are so few of them); but the chemists are the most expensive and insatiable among the expensive and insatiable. Moreover, their organizations can always produce at an instant's notice a set of national comparisons to support their case: no sooner, for instance, do you raise the stipends for their graduate students than they come up with a new survey that shows it wasn't enough. Chemists are particularly insatiable over the matter of journal subscriptions: they can't be competitive unless the library subscribes to every journal and has a complete back run of every journal; moreover, the library must be in the chemistry department, or next to it and open 24 hours a day, 365 (or 366) days per year, or if that is not the case then every member of the chemistry staff (including graduate students) must have a key to the library for instant access to the journals.

Chemists cannot be competitive without graduate students to work in their labs. In some departments, the rivalry among the faculty to attract graduate students to their own projects is so fierce that various regulations have been tried to keep dissension within some sort of bounds: for example, that no professor may have more than ten graduate students unless every other professor has at least two; or, that every entering graduate student must talk with every prospective thesis supervisor before actually choosing one. The situation is nicely illustrated by a tale that is supposed not to be apocryphal:

Professor Smith had a very able graduate student, Jones, who—like all good graduate students—spent all his waking time and some of his sleeping time in the lab. But at the annual departmental picnic, he was espied and coveted and seduced by Professor Smith's wife (whose husband also was wont to spend all his waking and much of his sleeping time in the lab). Poor Jones lost his sense of values and left town with Mrs. Smith, his research and his dissertation uncompleted. Some months later, a rumor ran around the department that Jones had applied for readmission, that Professor Smith was sponsoring his application and was willing again to supervise Jones's work. One of Smith's colleagues told him of the rumor and asked whether it could be true. "Yes, of course," responded Smith, "you know how it is. It's easy to find a wife, but good grad students are hard to come by."

*   *   *   *   *

The biologists don't quite know how to handle their supposed transition from descriptive natural historians to molecular-biological physicists and engineers who are about to displace the nuclear physicists in the political corridors of power. They're not even sure that "biology" exists, for that matter, or what kinship there is exactly among biochemists, botanists, ecologists, geneticists, microbiologists, molecular biologists, and zoologists, to name only a few of the subtribes. They have mixed feelings about and mixed relations with the faculties in agriculture, dentistry, medicine, veterinary science. Some people in those other colleges admittedly do good work, but they all enjoy unfair advantages. The aggies get a lot of research money from federal and state governments; they don't have to write research proposals and wouldn't be competitive if they did; they teach almost not at all and don't publish nearly as much as they ought to, considering the advantages they have. The medically related people are grossly overpaid and are not really scientists.

The geologists too don't quite know how to handle the transition of their subject from theoryless description to powerful physical and mathematical modeling. They're still a bit embarrassed that Wegener's theory of continental drift was rejected for so long. Some geologists are "really" chemists, and others are "really" physicists, but internecine warfare in geology departments is relatively (N.B. *relatively*) slight—perhaps because the departments tend to be rather small, feel somewhat threatened by the other, larger science departments, and therefore practice putting on a united front to the outside.

The B.S. in geology is becoming less guarantee of a job, the M.S. likewise for those with aspirations for research. The market for graduates behaves like a yo-yo, driven by the vagaries of chance—that is, federal energy policy and the policies of oil companies and Middle Eastern governments.

In the sciences, but especially in chemistry and in physics, "pure" is very different indeed from "applied." (In biology, the "applieds" are largely in agriculture or medicine, so the division has little practical consequence within biology departments.) The particle physicists rule the roost, being entirely "pure"; uniquely among purists, they get almost all the federal and other funds to which they believe themselves entitled. The physical chemists regard themselves as of equal stature, but nobody else does: they get no grants, no one wants to hire them, consequently they get few graduate students and even fewer good ones. In retaliation, the physical chemists seek to ensure that no one can pass their courses who is not already an accomplished mathematician or mathematical physicist. In those unfortunate departments where the physical chemists achieved power, analytical chemistry was soon dispensed with, and inorganic and organic chemistry were next on the hit list; and the freshman courses were upgraded and modernized so that no students could pass them unless they were already accomplished mathematicians or mathematical physicists.

The "applieds" rant and rave about this upside-down sense of status. Apart from the particle physicists, it is they who get almost all the grants, who support most of the graduate students and post-docs, and whose "overhead" keeps their departments going, yet their opinions are not wanted in matters of curriculum or promotion or departmental policy. But deep inside, the "applieds" actually share the same sense of values and know their enterprise to be truly inferior to that of the "pures." That is seen perhaps most clearly when people from industrial labs visit a university: the "applied" visitors are always intensely embarrassed about their natty clothes, salaries, lab facilities, and so on, and use every opportunity to indicate in subtle and not-so-subtle ways that their hearts are really in the right (pure) place, that at the earliest opportunity they will get back into academic work.

The Social Sciences

Historians are not quite sure whether they belong here or among the humanists. To me, it is evident that they belong in the humanities because—already by virtue of the name—sociology is the paradigmatic[5] social science; and I have never encountered a historian who would for a moment be mistaken for a sociologist, or vice versa. Political science has quite a few similarities with sociology, but there are fewer points of similarity with some of the oddments that are occasionally also lumped, for convenience,[6] in the social science category: anthropology, communications, geography, journalism, and so forth.

Don't ever ask sociologists what the latest exciting results in their field are, what problems have been solved, or what questions have been answered. The subject doesn't deal in answers or results, it deals only in approaches, both methodological and theoretical. The closest to excitement that you will see in social scientists comes when their computers' speed and memory are increased: more variables can then be handled, more data bases accommodated, and people in other places will be green with envy. To most natural scientists, "number-crunching" is a pejorative term; to many social scientists, it is the epitome of their endeavors.

Social scientists believe that *everything* is determined by totally political processes. Therefore they will gladly swell their ranks by accepting as colleagues anyone who promises to make common cause in the never-ending struggle to have social science recognized as legitimate, prestigious, valuable, and fully equal in every way to *real* science.[7] Perhaps that is why the large philosophy department in one of the large state universities is classed, for local purposes, among the social sciences.

Or perhaps those philosophers were welcomed not only for the votes they could bring but because of the penchant for theory and the theoretical that philosophers display: for in the true social sciences, theories abound, indeed they swamp everything else. In the humanities, everyone is supposed at some time to generate a book, but in the social sciences everyone is expected to generate a new theory—the broader-gauge and more all-encompassing the better. That is consistent, of course, with the fact that the field does not deal in answers or results. Every neophyte feels called upon to produce opuses that improve on Durkheim or Marx (which in one sense is admittedly not such a difficult task); I once heard such a theory described as "transcendental pragmatism" and have tried unsuccessfully ever since to put the term out of my mind. Not only do the social scientists indulge in barbarous jargon and neologisms, they also cannot spell: their articles are not refereed but "referred"; and when they have a tenure track, it has apparently two dimensions and not just one, since they call it a tenure "tract."

Sociologists avoid like the plague expressing anything resembling a definite opinion or conclusion; and that may partly explain why they never use a single word where a hundred will serve. So also nothing else is ever redundant for them: a serious study of what happens to articles rejected for publication in journals of social science revealed that most commonly they were expanded and published as books. Be warned, by the way, that in the social sciences "book" and "monograph" do not mean the same as in other fields; often the products are more like inhouse adult-education pamphlets or final reports to funding agencies.

A dean is supposed once to have confided that, because funds were so short, he had chosen mathematics as the field in which his college should truly seek excellence: "It's so cheap," he said. "Apart from the salaries you only have to buy the faculty desks and chairs, chalkboards and chalk, paper and wastebaskets." Another dean went him one better: "We've chosen sociology, which is even cheaper because they don't need the wastebaskets."

*   *   *   *   *

In some respects psychology fits the stereotype of social science, in other respects not; perhaps it is to mark that difference that the terms "behavioral" science and "cognitive" science have been introduced. Psychology too has a multitude of competing paradigms; but—by contrast with the sociologists—this does not temper the dogmatism of any given psychologist about the correctness of his particular paradigmatic view. Those views range from the most extreme sort of mechanistic materialist determinism (Skinnerian behaviorism) to the rankest mysticism; latterly, the philosophers of science have even declared psychoanalysis to be a pseudoscience.

No academic discipline is particularly noted for being insightful about itself; and there are the notorious oddities, for instance, how frequently mathematicians are not very good at calculating. But psychology may be the most extreme example, in that psychologists tend to be uncommonly bad judges of human nature. Perhaps it was not always like that, before psychology took the behaviorist stance which rules out of consideration all the factors that might differentiate human beings from other creatures.

The Humanities

It has often been remarked that professors in the humanities may not exemplify the virtues that are supposed to accrue from study of their subjects. Perhaps the undoubtedly real and long neglect of those disciplines and of their practitioners has stimulated the attitude of cynical bitterness that I encountered here so much more often than in other fields. I guess the humanists are about as other-directed as are the social scientists, and may therefore and without quite knowing it have come themselves to accept the low value that society appears to place on their enterprise. But many humanists can still express themselves beautifully; and since my own sense of humor also tends to the sardonic and sarcastic, I derived much (albeit quite private) enjoyment from the sallies that our humanists ventured at nonhumanists, at each other, at their students, at their chairs, and at me.

Historians impressed me most often with their comprehensive and erudite knowledge and understanding of people and society and circumstance, of connections and relationships; unfortunately, any given historian displays such understanding with respect to circumstances only in one country (or part of a country) during a period of rarely more than a few decades. Thus our history department had more courses by far in its catalog listing than any other department—some 150 supposedly distinct and different "offerings," as I recall. And prestige attached to teaching tiny groups of seniors or graduate students, not the huge numbers who enrolled in the introductory and survey courses.

In one respect, many historians resemble sociologists: they don't like to be vulnerable to the charge of having made an unqualified assertion about a specific topic within their field. With the sociologists, the reluctance stems no doubt from their penchant for offering sweeping theoretical generalizations; whereas with the historians, it reflects a recognition that their work is always incomplete, that the discovery tomorrow of an artifact or document could *prove* them wrong.

Historians, as all the rest of us, acknowledge that science and technology have crucially influenced our culture, especially over the last few centuries. Yet historians have not incorporated those influences into their teaching of intellectual or social history; and they continue to treat history of science and history of technology as disciplines separate from "history" itself. In many places, the historians of medicine, science, and technology are in separate departments or institutes; where one or two or three of them find themselves in history departments, they all too rarely feel genuinely at home. Part of the difficulty stems from the typically different education of the historian of science: an undergraduate degree in a science followed by graduate work in a separate department of history of science. Over the last decade or two, a strikingly large number of women have become interested in these fields, and programs in the history of medicine, science, or technology have hired many intellectually first-rate women.

I was saddened by the lack of generosity that humanists often display toward colleagues, especially in English and the various language departments. Almost all of their undergraduate students are taught by graduate students or by instructors not on the tenure track;[8] the "real" professors take the supposedly more interesting and prestigious upper-level undergraduate classes and all the graduate courses. In return, the non-tenure-tracked are given no thanks; rather the opposite: every opportunity seems to be taken to make clear that they belong to the lowest caste, for instance, by not inviting them to participate in departmental faculty meetings. The supposedly substantive root of some of this differentiation lies in the fact that much of the undergraduate course-work is intended to produce skill in written or oral use of a language, whereas the "real" work of those disciplines lies, again supposedly, in literary criticism.

Some of the downtrodden have realized that the rest of society thinks the ability to write to be more important than a deep appreciation of the use of metaphor in James Joyce, say, and a band of entrepreneurs has been forming to gain separate and professional status for "teaching of composition." And that band has also laid claim to the future by embracing the use of computers—or at least by talking about using computers. But once again, the very stridency of these entrepreneurs may indicate that, other-directed as they also are, they too accept as actually valid the traditional hierarchy in which they are at the bottom, below the editors who are perhaps below, perhaps above, or perhaps on a par with the bibliographers, all of whom are well below the literary critics. The people who actually write the stuff upon which all these troops feed, by the way, have no status at all. Poets and novelists may be given brief visiting appointments, so that they can be studied "in the wild," so to speak; but let a member of the faculty actually write poems or novels or short stories, and he is looked upon askance. It is bad form for academics to write literature rather than about literature.[9]

The rest of academe seems to lump together all professors of all foreign languages as being somehow essentially the same; that is anything but the view taken from the inside, however. There are more subtribes here than there are separate languages (for each language has its language teachers and its literature professors; and then there are the comparative linguists); and the mutual estrangements can be as deep and hostile as they are among the nations that speak those languages. Where there exist departments encompassing more than one language, typically there is a formal organization into divisions, each with its own chair or coordinator and its committees on curriculum and personnel in particular. Everywhere each group wants to have its own department, and some of the smallest departments in most universities are those representing the less popular languages.

The pecking order among language departments has long been in flux. In Europe the classics ruled the roost at one time, but in the United States languages seem to have been established primarily in deference to their possible vocational functions. So departmental fortunes wax and wane with international affairs and economics: German is in very bad shape; French is nothing like what it used to be; Russian has declined drastically from its brief but glorious heyday; Spanish feels itself to be the wave of the future, and it is indeed the tidal wave of the present.

Professors of the less common languages periodically turn optimistic when someone in Washington or at a foundation calls for attention to the many languages of countries with which we must deal; very infrequently, however, are such calls accompanied by wherewithal. That dealing with China or Japan is important to us does not bring students flocking to learn those languages; and few universities will long support scholars in fields that attract no students.

The philosophers surprised me by coupling the most subtle and rigorous logic within their discipline to extraordinary illogicality on all other matters. I often wondered about the origin of "philosophical" as applied to temperament, since I rarely met a philosopher who exemplified that; rather, the philosophers seem to rival the artists and the pure mathematicians in propensity to explode even without overt provocation. While the other humanists deplore the ignorance of the masses who do not recognize the lasting value of the content of the humanistic disciplines, the philosophers are uncomfortable because they have themselves discovered, through work within their discipline, that large parts of philosophy no longer exist, for example, moral philosophy or political philosophy. So they are trying to recapture the good old days of natural philosophy by turning more and more to philosophy of science. So far, the scientists themselves have shown no signs of appreciating this move.

My education had prepared me to admire humanists as those who keep alive the flame of culture even through ages of darkness, and I often felt badly about the doldrums in which the humanities seem to find themselves. But I also think that the humanists themselves are partly responsible, as I once tried to explain:

"I've grown tired of hearing about the lack of support for the humanities. I'm tired not because I am against support for the humanities but because the complaints are so clearly self-serving; and because the arguments are so weak; but chiefly because I detect a lack of true conviction and a lack of self-respect in the complaining voices. We claim that the humanities are central, essential, even ultimately useful to human beings. But what have our own actions said?

"During the 1960s—and we haven't changed much since— our actions said that students could judge no less well than could mature scholars what is fundamental and what should be in a curriculum. Our actions said that years and decades spent in scholarship and teaching gave us no right to determine what students should study. What can we now convincingly claim to be valuable about studying and writing and learning to share our knowledge, when we didn't claim to have gained understanding or a measure of wisdom from our life in academe?

"Our actions said that the study of a foreign language is not particularly meaningful.

"Our actions said that we would take students into college no matter how ill prepared they were.

"Our actions said that it was all right in a university to teach remedial English and remedial mathematics.

"And our actions continue to say that money is most precious to us. The life of the mind is OK just so long as the salaries are high; we will spend the summer on our scholarly work just so long as we get a stipend for it.

"It is against those actions that the present complaints sound so weak to me. The voters and the people in Congress are increasingly those who were our students in the years when we told them that they were already as wise as we! I simply don't believe that our complaints will now carry much weight with them. We must first recapture our convictions and we must act out of those convictions. And when we do that, the respect and the support will come.

"We express dissatisfaction at the difficulty of getting grants, compared to the supposed ease of doing so in the sciences; at the disparities in salaries, graduate fellowships, travel money, and so on. Well, the sciences have that support because scientists really believe that knowledge, understanding, and wisdom belong to them, and they project that belief so unashamedly, wholeheartedly, arrogantly even, that the wider society simply has to agree. Scientists tell their students—and did so throughout the sixties and seventies—exactly what to study, in considerable detail—no nonsense about choosing any one of a couple of dozen available options. And scientists project the image of Martin Arrowsmith and Albert Einstein, to whom nothing was more important than their work which benefited all humankind.

"So, I suggest, the humanities will be respected, valued, and held in awe only when scholars do likewise. When they take strong stands on their knowledge and understanding, when they treat students as students and apprentices, when they put their work first. And when they are prepared to do that, the task may turn out to be easier than they ever dreamed. Think of the awe in which Robert Oppenheimer was held, and then remember how frequently we were reminded of his knowledge of Sanskrit, his reading of poetry, his *nonscientific* understanding. Try to imagine what could happen if, with full conviction, you were to show your students that psychology and sociology and political science and much else can be learned best from Chaucer and Shakespeare and Dickens and Shaw. Imagine what could happen if you insisted that writing cannot be good unless the thinking is clear, and that whole bureaucracies can be swept aside if only their jargon is punctured and rejected firmly and consistently.

"I happen to believe that the humanities are central, essential, and even useful to human beings. And I eagerly await the time when humanists join me in that belief and act on it."

*   *   *   *   *

Tribal attitudes on some matters can be treated by topic more conveniently than by discipline:

Textbooks

Academics are unanimous across all disciplines that people who author textbooks should get no credit for it. If those authors happen not to get particularly high evaluations from the students in their classes, for example, then those evaluations take precedence and the authors are ranked low on "contributions to instruction" no matter how widely or well adopted their texts may be. And of course textbooks don't count as "publications," because the latter means only *research* publications. The national visibility that accrues to the authors of widely adopted texts (everybody in the field knows their names and where they work) does not count as national visibility for purposes of tenure or promotion, and wouldn't count for the purpose of salary raises if the faculty had any say in that.

These attitudes are sometimes supported by pointing out that authors of texts get their reward in royalties,[10] and it would be inequitable—sort of "double dipping"—to give them raises and tenure as well. But fundamentally the reasoning runs that textbooks are not research (my faculty would not even agree to call them works of "scholarship"), and only research counts.

I learned quite quickly as dean that "publish or perish" is not mandated by administrators but by the community of the faculty themselves, who simply will not count (dare I say countenance?) pedagogical effort or achievement as worthwhile.[11]

Graduate Students

In the sciences, graduate students are apprentices who ideally have become full-fledged partners of their professors by the time they graduate. The work is shared always; at first and inevitably, however, the professor provides almost all the judgment and the student contributes only the physical work. Joint publication is normal as well as justified, and individual attitudes determine in which order the authors' names are listed: some professors always use alphabetical order, others try to list by degree of contribution to the work (with the main contributor first), some always put their names first, and some practice the reverse snobbery of always placing their names last.

Humanists and mathematicians do not usually work jointly with their graduate students. Most commonly their students choose topics independently and work at them with only occasional and often only general advice from their "major professor." Since the work is not joint, the student usually publishes alone.

The social sciences are, in this respect at least, more akin to the sciences, but they make a much more elaborate fuss about the order of the authors' names on the publications.

In the sciences, some graduate students get financial support from grants, usually grants obtained by their major professors. There are fewer such opportunities in the social sciences or in the mathematical sciences, and they are virtually unknown in the humanities or the arts.

Most graduate students are supported by teaching assistantships; in the sciences, they supervise undergraduate labs. Scientists are incredulous that in the other fields graduate students are actually allowed to teach lecture courses. Scientists are also incredulous that in the other fields graduate students supported on teaching assistantships are often assigned to help professors with grading and even with odd jobs useful to the professor's own research.

Going into Administration

All academics are hostile toward administrators, but the degree of hostility varies among the disciplines:

MOST HOSTILE	English
	Political Science
	Sociology
	Other humanities and social sciences
	Mathematical sciences
	Natural sciences
LEAST HOSTILE	Fine, dramatic, and musical arts

The least hostile, of course, are those who are most engaged in their creative or scholarly pursuits, and vice versa. The artists display hostility toward no one, by the way (except toward their immediate colleagues, that is). The most hostile are contemptuous not only of administrators but also of academe as a whole, their own disciplinary profession, and even themselves.[12]

It is also worth remarking that those who are the most hostile toward administrators are at the same time those who themselves most want to become administrators. Thus in English, political science, or sociology, one who becomes an administrator is regarded by colleagues as having crowned a career with success; whereas in the sciences, a turning to administration is seen as the mark of failure, or at least as the end of one's career. For the artists, administration is an entirely unthinkable task, as illustrated by the behavior of those artists who find themselves with an administrative title.

The urge to try a hand at administration strikes people at different ages in the different disciplines, consonant with whether such a move is supposed to mark failure or success: thus in English or in political science or in sociology, youngsters who have just—or even not yet—attained tenure feel ready to be chosen as administrators; whereas in the sciences, the urge to take up administering usually comes as part of the mid-life crisis.

In all fields, the ambition to administrate is seen at an earlier age in women than in men.

Overall Support: Salaries, Research Funds, Travel Money, and So On

The scientists know that the world owes them support, because eventually the world gets more from science in return.

The social scientists say that the world owes them equally such support, because it would eventually get at least as much in return as from the sciences; but the social scientists don't really believe that when they say it, and certainly no one else does.

The mathematical scientists are at least three separate tribes: the computer scientists get more support than is warranted, but they think just the opposite to be the case; the pure mathematicians get all the support they need or could use, but think they should ask for more just for equity's sake; the applied mathematicians and the statisticians find much of their own support and thus earn their keep.

The humanists try to convince themselves that, if not the world, then at least their own university owes them a living (and some loving).

The artists are incredulous that anyone lets them survive, let alone gives them any support.

Notes

1. A term I've appropriated from the delightful book by Hazard Adams, *The Academic Tribes*, New York: Liveright, 1976; rev. ed., Urbana & Chicago: University of Illinois Press, 1988.

2. In addition to the just cited book by Adams, I dare to draw attention to the following as worth reading: Jacques Barzun, *Teacher in America*, Boston: Little, Brown, 1945; Garden City, N.Y.: Doubleday Anchor Books, 1954; *The House of Intellect*, London: Secker & Warburg, 1959; London: Mercury Books, 1962; and *The American University*, New York, Evanston & London: Harper & Row, 1968; F. M. Cornford, *Microcosmographia Academica*, Cambridge: Bowes & Bowes, 1908; Oliver P. Kolstoe, *College Professoring*, Carbondale & Edwardsville: Southern Illinois University Press, 1975; Academicus Mentor, *Up the Ivy*, New York: Hawthorn, 1966; Professor X, *Never at a Loss for an Opinion*, New Rochelle, N.Y.: Arlington House, 1974; John R. Searle, *The Campus War*, New York & Cleveland: World Publishing, 1971; Harmondsworth (Middlesex): Pelican (Penguin), 1972; Pierre van den Berghe, *Academic Gamesmanship*, London, New York & Toronto: Abelard-Schuman, 1970.

Some works of fiction have captured salient bits of the feel of academe, for instance, Hazard Adams, *The Horses of Instruction*, New York: Harcourt, Brace & World, 1968; Kingsley Amis, *Lucky Jim*, London: Gollancz, 1953; Nigel Balchin, *A Sort of Traitors*, London: Collins, 1949; Malcolm Bradbury, *The History Man*, London: Secker & Warburg, 1975; William Cooper, *The Struggles of Albert Woods*, London: Jonathan Cape, 1952; Randall Jarrell, *Pictures from an Institution*, New York: Knopf, 1954; David Lodge, *Changing Places*, London: Secker & Warburg, 1975; Alison Lurie, *The War between the Tates*, New York: Random House, 1974; Mary McCarthy, *The Groves of Academe*, New York: Harcourt, Brace & World, 1951.

3. Anne Roe, *The Making of a Scientist*, New York: Dodd, Mead, 1952.

4. Innumeracy is to numbers what illiteracy is to letters. Just as illiterates speak and write without realizing their own incoherence, so innumerates construct budgets and do arithmetic without realizing that their numbers make no sense.

5. It may, of course, be paradoxical to talk of a "paradigmatic" social science since these subjects, collectively and individually, have no paradigms in the sense that the sciences do—or have a multitude of them, at least several to each subfield or subtribe. But then much else is also paradoxical about the social sciences (even apart from the term itself).

6. It is not often enough understood that such arrangements "purely for convenience" almost inevitably make for great *incon*venience or even worse.

7. The social scientists actually want only the appurtenances of this recognition: they themselves do not regard their enterprise as being truly science. At an early meeting of the Society for Social Studies of Science, which had been founded largely by political scientists and sociologists of science, a speaker asked those in the audience of about 150 to raise their hands who were themselves or had been "scientists": only a few hands went up, from erstwhile engineers or physicists. The "social scientists" present simply did not think of themselves as just plain "scientists," no matter how loudly they might in other settings protest that they should be so regarded by others.

8. See, for example, Kurt Heinzelman, "The English Lecturers at Austin: Our New M.I.A.'s," *Academe*, January-February 1986, 25–31.

9. I have it on good authority that I'm behind the times as regards the creative writers: they now exert power while continuing to complain that they have none.

10. Getting money from publication is a sure sign that the publication is without true value. Faculty are proud when their books can only be published if the publishers are reimbursed beforehand for the financial loss that publication will entail. More than one humanist told me with a straight face what honor would come to the college and the university from the note on the copyright page of his book, that publication had been supported by the institution. I could never understand that, since such publications incur a loss only because almost no one ever has the interest to read them, and thus very few people would ever know that we had borne part of the costs.

11. A paradox: take half-a-dozen individuals, each a conscientious teacher as well as researcher, put them together as a committee to evaluate others, and they will agree that textbooks should not count. They will also agree that "the administration" does not—but should—reward teaching.

12. See, for example, *Confessions of an American Scholar*, Minneapolis: University of Minnesota Press, 1970, by Simon O'Toole (pseud.), a professor of English.

17

Tricks of the Trade

"Your job is mainly one of educating," the V-P said to me once, during a conversation more general and less hurried than usual.

I hadn't thought about it in that way before; but the more I considered it, the more useful an insight it seemed to me. I had already realized much earlier, it is true, that deans have no actual power that they can effectively exercise—not often or for long, anyway—just by telling others what to do; their power resides rather in having ready access to many people at all levels, giving them the opportunity to persuade and to arrange co-operations, greatly assisted in that by the widespread illusion that deans actually have a great deal of power which they wield ruthlessly and even capriciously.[1] So I'd seen my job as one of educating in the sense of persuading, but the V-P meant it more literally than that and thus had a deeper insight for me.

The dean's role is unique: he has a unique view in all directions, and some experiences quite unlike those that come to other administrators. Deans need not only to represent their colleges, they must—even to do that effectively—*interpret* their colleges to the V-P, to the rest of the central administration, to all the middle-management bureaucrats, and indeed to their own staff and chairs and faculty, for no one else really *cares* about the college as such and as a whole, and no one else can really appreciate the problems of caring for and about such an enterprise.

By contrast, chairs have little educating that only they can do: the faculty know almost as much as they do that is germane. Perhaps chairs can explain to faculty a little about the college and about the dean, but they don't themselves understand those all that well. Chairs can try to educate deans about their departments and their disciplines, but deans can and must learn some of that from others too.

The vice-president can try to educate the deans, but really only about nonacademic and therefore ephemeral and uninteresting things: the latest from the board of governors, general financial outlooks, things of that sort; anything of lasting value that the V-P knows was probably acquired during a term as chair or dean. The V-P can of course try to educate the rest of the central administration about academic matters, but that always strikes me as close to a hopeless venture or a lost cause: those in central administration who haven't been professors and then chairs or deans themselves will likely never be able to understand properly.

So deans hold the highest administrative post[2] in which one still learns things that have a useful relationship to the substantive content of the academic disciplines and to the task of helping them develop or seeing that their development is not hindered. And so deans come to have significant insights that are not vouchsafed to others, and have the opportunity, indeed the responsibility, to educate those others.

*   *   *   *   *

One of the major shocks for me came when I was forced to recognize that most of the middle managers—accountants, personnel officers, and the like—genuinely do not care about the academic side of things; that is, paradoxical as it may appear, they really don't care about the raison d'être of the business in which they are engaged.[3] Not that there is normally much deliberate malice or sabotage; it is just that they simply don't understand intellect, and therefore they don't understand what it takes to make an environment intellectually attractive, and they do not accept that this has to be the top priority to which everything else—including "efficiency" as usually and narrowly defined—must be subordinated. The accountants want their operation to run efficiently *from its own point of view,* no matter how inconvenient and therefore inefficient that may make things for the faculty or the students; the people in admissions and registration want their operations to be efficient *from their point of view,* no matter how inconvenient and therefore inefficient that may be for the faculty and the students and how damaging to the goal of recruiting the best students; and so on. The rarely understood point is that all such offices should be *in*efficient from their own point of view in order to conserve the time and the peace of mind of the faculty, which are the most precious and irreplaceable assets of any university, and in order to emphasize to students that concentration on academic matters is what is expected of them. Although accounting and admissions offices and computing centers and so on are often referred to as "service" units, in practice they are not commonly made actually to function as units whose only proper role is to serve the academic enterprise.[4]

Thinking of efficiency narrowly, and commonly only in terms of the most directly visible expenditure, can have extraordinary consequences. Thus when telephone costs began their disastrously steep climb, our director of communications let it be known that we could easily enjoy better service at lower cost. Though I was skeptical, it seemed at least conceivable that high technology might, at last and in this instance at least, be able actually to deliver on one of its promises. So we accepted the director's offer to explain his scheme to us in detail.

"Look," he told us, "the deans' offices have half-a-dozen multiconnection phones, which are very expensive; and the secretaries spend a lot of their time answering those phones and then putting the calls through to the people who actually need to answer them. Take out those systems, and give every dean and associate dean and assistant dean one ordinary phone, and let them answer it directly themselves and save everybody's time."

Except their own, I tried to explain, but he was impervious—since he answered his own phone himself, he couldn't understand why everyone else shouldn't do the same; he just couldn't grasp that most of the calls to a dean's office should *not* be answered by the dean.[5] So we had a stalemate, which I finally resolved with a suggestion that I tried to make in a neutral tone: "Well, sir, perhaps you're right. I'll tell you what: if the president's office accepts your approach and the president takes to answering his own phone, do let me know and we'll do the same in these offices."

I never heard from him again.

His successor as director of communications had the computer disease. He wanted to see a terminal on every desk, so that communication could be instantaneous. He didn't seem to understand my response: why should the college spend such vast sums of money, both capital expenditure and running costs, just to make it even easier for everybody to be incessantly interrupted? Telephones are surely a rapid enough mode of communication when rapidity is needed. For most matters, a day or two in the campus mail causes no harm. And moreover, what would happen if we followed his urging, replaced the telephones and internal campus mail entirely by these terminals, and then found ourselves periodically without any means of communication at all when the computer was "down"?

But, like all these enthusiasts,[6] he couldn't bring himself to admit that the computer ever crashed. Or perhaps he just regarded that as a price that everyone ought to be willing to pay in return for being at the cutting edge of modernity. Certainly he seemed to regard as impolite any mention of defects or weaknesses in computing, be it in principle or in the system actually in place on our campus.

*   *   *   *   *

Though all administrators ought to have been professors first (and, indeed, ought always to *remain* professors first), in a couple of respects teaching and research are poor preparation for administrative duties.

Professors do things themselves, and are able to get appropriate satisfaction directly from things they've done: the draft of a paper written brings a sense of achievement; the last filling in of grades at the end of a semester, too, brings the sense that one has done something, that some students at least have been helped. But administrators never do anything directly useful; their possible utility resides in enabling or persuading others to do useful things. And because others are always involved, administrators can rarely take much satisfaction from their own contributions, which in any event are rarely identifiable. Professors can often say of their research, and sometimes of their teaching, "If it hadn't been for me personally, this wouldn't have been done, or at least not so well." The dean can very rarely say of something well done in teaching or research, "This would not have happened if *I personally* had not been dean." Thus professors who become administrators must learn, with little or no preparation for it, to derive satisfaction vicariously from the achievements of others.

Professors, like many people who actually themselves do substantive things, rightly learn that procrastination is bad: "Never leave until the morrow, that which you can do today." But much that comes to a chair or a dean is best handled by doing nothing at all, or by only pretending to do something, and innumerable other matters are better handled slowly than promptly. I found that a very difficult thing to learn and had to keep reminding myself of it, for habits acquired early are hard to shake later— like being taught as a child never to leave anything uneaten on one's plate, which becomes dangerous to health in middle age. At any rate, too prompt an administrator can produce havoc. My in-tray would occasionally deliver up something like the following:

TO: Dean Martin
FROM: Vice-President for Administration
SUBJECT: Traffic Violation by State Vehicle

On or about March 29, a state vehicle was allowed to stand, contrary to indicated regulations, for an unknown length of time but at least thirty (30) minutes, in front of the Department of Journalism. Investigation has revealed that the vehicle in question had been signed out to Dr. Halifax. Pursuant to the official procedures, this memorandum requests that an interview be arranged with Dr. Halifax, that he be apprised of the serious nature of such breaches of the regulations, particularly involving state vehicles, that his written recognition of the seriousness of the breach and assurance of future compliance be obtained and documented to this office.

Halifax happened to be one of our more distinguished faculty, holder of an endowed chair. Moreover, in my view he genuinely and amply deserved his distinctions: he lived and breathed his subject and was always fascinating when he talked about it. He had for a time practiced in the real world of newspapers, but that was long ago; he had also long ago discarded whatever respect he might once have had for such practicalities of life as parking regulations. As with many of our faculty of distinction, his ego bruised rather easily, and anything less than a resounding compliment or total agreement with his opinion caused him to wonder whether he was no longer fully appreciated; any slight actual criticism sent him for days into a huff during which he composed, and even sent, extraordinarily long letters to everyone from his chair through the dean to the vice-president and the president.

What useful purpose could be served by attempting to make Halifax jump through hoops about parking regulations?

Now recall that deans do not get fired for entirely ignoring such requests from the Office of the Vice-President for Administration, which makes that one possible and even attractive course of (in)action. But one doesn't want to acquire too great a reputation for being an un-member of the administrative team, and besides, one all too often needs something from the Office of the Vice-President for Administration. The best approach, therefore, is to change one's pace and manner of operation[7] from that of doing things, and promptly, to the different manner that characterizes, for instance, such offices as that of the vice-president for administration. What does the V-P do when one of your departments needs a new roof to stop the rain from ruining millions of dollars worth of equipment (which the V-P has also refused to insure against such catastrophes)? The V-P sends long, smarmy, evasive memos, that's what. So:

TO: Vice-President for Administration
FROM: Dean Martin
SUBJECT: Traffic Violation by State Vehicle
This office appreciates having its attention drawn to this matter. The serious nature of the offense is fully recognized, as is the need to ensure that nothing of a similar nature again eventuates. Appropriate action will be devised and implemented, and the chair of the department will be asked for appropriate advice not only for handling this instance but for appropriate future planning and action. Perhaps some clearer understandings should be developed of the frequency and appropriateness of the need of the faculty to avail themselves of the privilege of the use of state vehicles.
Rest assured that the matter will be handled just as it should be.

Having sent that, or something like it, you should then *do nothing else.* If you ever receive a reminder or follow-up from the V-P, which is quite unlikely, respond to it again in similar fashion. You can always mention the difficulty of scheduling an appointment with Halifax, who is always off-campus at conferences and who breaks appointments with the dean at the drop of a hat; the V-P will readily believe that, since he thinks he knows how little time most faculty actually spend at work.

*   *   *   *   *

Quite often, what may superficially seem to be requests that you take action are really nothing of the sort. Chairs as well as deans get many visits from individual professors who come to complain of this, that, and the other. Almost invariably there is nothing that could conceivably be done: the professors have simply collided with some aspect of reality—the universal need for more money, say, or the incalcitrance of some of their colleagues, or some corollary of the professor's own self-doubt. Administrators should be clear that *they are doing something,* indeed doing all that it is possible to do, *simply by listening* to Professor Q, by sympathizing, by musing about possible courses of action, by sharing the ridiculous complexities that any administrative action entails, and by urging Professor Q to come back at any time. For professors, talking may often be mutually exclusive of doing, but for administrators that is not the case.

Deans have to deal with people, and they have to deal with issues; both sorts of dealings can be facilitated by following a few maxims. In dealing with people, to preserve good relations for as long as possible, never write a memo when it is possible instead to talk about the matter at hand. By all means follow up the talk with a memo, for the record or to specify details; but anything that could be misunderstood—and almost anything can and will be—and anything that can arouse ire—and almost anything can and will—is handled more effectively, with more good fellowship and good will, if you first make a personal approach. Face-to-face, one is less likely to attribute unworthy motives to people with whom one disagrees. That one should pause before jumping to conclusions about the motives of others is pithily expressed in one of my favorite injunctions:

NEVER ATTRIBUTE TO MALICE

WHAT CAN BE EXPLAINED BY INCOMPETENCE

because incompetence really is so much more common than deliberate malice.

I did not myself keep that maxim sufficiently at the forefront of my mind and invariably regretted the lapse soon thereafter. All too often I became angry through jumping to the false conclusion that some preposterous absurdity or other was known by the perpetrator to be a preposterous absurdity. In the attempt to curb my tendency to be undiplomatic on those occasions, I made a little placard to keep on my desk. I heartily recommend these rules to those who share my low boiling point:

DESTROY THE FIRST DRAFT

RESPOND TO THE MANIFEST, NOT TO AN INTERPRETATION OF IT

CRITICIZE THE ACTION IF NEED BE, BUT NOT THE ACTOR

IS THIS MEMO NECESSARY? WHAT CAN IT ACHIEVE?

Of course, if it cannot achieve anything more useful than blowing off deanly steam, don't send it.

Quite generally, deans need to exercise firm judgment in choosing what to take on and what to avoid. If it were left to others, deans would find their days full of things that don't particularly need doing—or even if they do, certainly not by deans. With respect to trivial matters that some misguided others did not recognize as trivial, I found it useful to bear in mind a motto that I learned in high school from a teacher of Latin:

ANYTHING UNNECESSARY IS *WRONG*

I have found that a marvelous guide in life generally, not only for the writing of good Latin, and notably after I became an administrator.

But there are many unnecessary things that a dean cannot avoid doing: preparing mission statements, for instance, or six-year plans to which subsequent appropriations and budgets bear no relationship whatever, not even semantic ones. For those situations, one can express much the same notion in a more practical way:

IF A THING IS NOT WORTH DOING,

THEN IT IS NOT WORTH DOING WELL

"Strategic planning" was one of the activities of which much was made but which I could not take very seriously. It is carried on at a level of abstraction that ignores the nuts and bolts[8] of the activity being planned for. I did not regard it as reassuring that people could be "experts" in strategic planning per se— just as I don't much care for management experts who claim to know how one can manage any activity at all without ever having partaken of it.[9] It is rather like the notion that has ruined the schools: that teachers need only know "how to teach" and not much or anything about the subjects to be taught. I found it curious also that many of the expert strategic planners had earlier been architects or urban planners. The concrete products that have come from those realms of activity would seem to provide scant warrant for trusting the expertise of the practitioners.

In any case, what is substantive in a university is the academic work of teaching and research, and the ever-present concern must be, which areas to support better and which not so well? And that is a question that cannot usefully be argued publicly, as evidenced by the innumerable places that have been in serious financial difficulties but failed to evolve an academically sound plan. If some colleges are to be treated preferentially over others, then it is up to the V-P to do it; within a college, it is the dean who must decide among the departments.

Once given that sort of overall view, all else immediately falls into place, because there are rarely or never enough discretionary funds at any one time to make possible any sort of "big splash." At any rate, my possibly[10] misguided contempt for strategic planning could be summarized as

WISE MEN DON'T NEED TO PLAN,

BECAUSE THEY KNOW WHAT TO DO

One of my mentors long ago gave me a print of Picasso's sketch of Don Quixote and urged me to hang it in a prominent place; he thought I had an unfortunate tendency to take up lost causes. A fine expression of the same warning was the message of the film *Wargames:*

A STRANGE GAME: THE ONLY WINNING MOVE IS NOT TO PLAY

I sometimes wished that our president and vice-presidents had recognized the wisdom of that, say, with respect to intercollegiate athletics or in response to the initiatives "in support [*sic*] of higher education" that were too often mooted by state and federal governments.

Unfortunately, I often heard arguments along the following lines: "We really must do so and so. After all, if we don't, then we'll be forced to."[11] For example, develop means for "outcomes assessment," one of the more recent fads emanating from theorists of educationism and welcomed by bureaucrats: the idea is to determine what benefit students have derived from their instruction by comparing their capabilities after graduating with those they possessed when entering—compare the economic concept of "value added." Until one tries to think of valid ways of measuring that benefit, the idea may not necessarily be recognized as silly.

But that whole line of reasoning—do something (or just pretend to do something) silly because otherwise you will be forced to do it in a perhaps even sillier way—presumes that universities cannot educate those who are no longer students: governors of states, for example, or their secretaries for education, or those on their staffs. I couldn't disagree more. Universities need to educate the legislators and governors to understand what universities are, for no one else will. I recall my horror when, about three decades ago, a legislator criticized the University of Michigan for being "less productive" than the other public colleges in that state—its ratio of students to faculty was lower. . . . That legislator ought to have been told:

EVEN THOUGH EDUCATION IS NOT-FOR-PROFIT,

YOU CAN'T GET SOMETHING FOR NOTHING

It may be true that

HE WHO PAYS THE PIPER, CALLS THE TUNE

but

HE CANNOT TEACH THE MUSICIANS HOW TO PLAY IT

It is simply the case that quality costs more than mediocrity.

If one compares universities with businesses or with government agencies, it should be evident that universities are incredibly efficient: professors are given the assistance, per capita, of much less in the way of secretarial services, office machinery, and the like; and their salaries are low in relation to other professions when one considers the length of training required. One rapid way of costing this out is to consider the rates charged by universities for indirect costs incurred in managing grants and contracts for research; those charged by private industry are about twice as much. But, of course, the facts notwithstanding, legislators will continue to call for belt-tightening and "managing down" and more accountability and so on.

*   *   *   *   *

So many weighty, serious matters come to a dean that the occasional pieces of light relief are most welcome. I found reminders of the following in my files.

One of our faculty brought me a communication he had received from one of the coaches. It was a form letter, into the blank spaces of which had been inserted the professor's name as addressee and into the text the name of a student athlete. I reproduce the form, without those names, as well as the memo it spawned:

TO: . . . .
FROM: Royle True, Head Basketball Coach
. . . . , one of our student-athletes, was called home due to a death in the family. He will check with you when he returns to class.
    If you have any questions, feel free to call me.

TO: Vice-President for Academic Affairs
FROM: Dean Martin
SUBJECT: Deaths of Relatives of Student Athletes
    Attached is a form letter used by the athletics department to notify instructors when basketball players have experienced a death in the family. I find it alarming that the death rate among that group should be so high as to require the use of a form letter for these occasions. After all, we only have 15 people on the basketball squad. If an appreciable number of their relatives die during the few years of the players' eligibility, then the death rate among relatives of members of our squad must exceed the death rate in the general population by a staggering factor.

The professor who had shown me that—and I—found less occasion to laugh a year or so later when he discovered in his mailbox a plain envelope, no return address, his name handwritten on the front, with four season tickets inside.

But, it turns out, athletes are not the only group whose relatives are at high risk. A careful study revealed that students who receive grades of D or F suffer disproportionately more misfortunes, including deaths of relatives, than do students who receive grades of A, B, or C; and it was postulated that the grades of D and F in fact *are caused by* these misfortunes over which the students have no control.[12] If athletes belong to the group of students who receive grades of D or F, then the form letter used by our coach may after all have been necessary.

*   *   *   *   *

Dear Dean Martin:

As you know, my colleague Peters is being recommended by this department for promotion to full professor. I was a member of the department's Committee on Evaluation, Tenure, and Promotion, and I supported his case and voted in favor. Peters is beginning to be professionally active again after a long hiatus, and I wanted to encourage him to continue in that direction. Of course, his credentials do not pass muster under our present criteria and standards, and I will understand if you do not support the promotion. Indeed, I don't think that Peters should be promoted.

John Q. Doever
Professor

*   *   *   *   *

Distinction in an academic specialty is not necessarily correlated with common sense or a sense of perspective. Some of my best friends might hold endowed chairs, but I wished occasionally that I could—or, as dean, could afford to—have the last word with them; however, the fun derived from bruising such an ego is hardly worth what it then takes to assuage the bruise. Perhaps my most cherished and reckless moment with a distinguished one came when he was as usual telling me how to do my job, on this occasion what offer I should extend to a particular candidate for a faculty position.

"But really," I said, "we're already offering a higher rank than his credentials warrant, and we're offering to match his salary which is much higher than it would be if he had been working at a university rather than in industry. You understand what grief I'm going to take over that from your colleagues for the next few years. He's simply being unreasonable by asking for yet more; some might even call it attempted blackmail."

The distinguished professor sighed; he always found it diffi-cult to make administrators grasp the obvious. "We're build-ing," he expostulated; "we've got no visibility yet. This is the best we can do at the moment. No one who is *really* good would come here."

Got him! "You came here, didn't you?" I asked, trying not to let my pleasure be too obnoxiously evident.

Notes

1. Probably I need to be more explicit here. A dean's power is very limited indeed to get anything done that is academically substantive and desirable. Like most administrators, of course, a dean has ample means to delay or block initiatives that come from faculty or depart-ments, even though those initiatives may be desirable ones. Unfor-tunately, a dean has much less the means to block or delay *un*desirable initiatives, because those usually come not from the departments but from the vice-president, the president, the board, or extraneous (ex-tra-university) sources.

It is the case that the dean has the power to make good things happen occasionally, but those are things of limited extent, often having sig-nificance for just one other individual at any given time. Nevertheless, I find even in retrospect that it is from actions of that sort that I still derive the most satisfaction, especially the few occasions when I threw all caution to the winds and then had to scramble to get the agreements that would permit my decision to stand. Though my satisfaction over those incidents is real, it would be entirely improper for me to tell of them; in some instances, indeed, the beneficial effect would be quite nullified were my part in the matter ever to become known.

The real power to accomplish academically substantive things resides in the departments, but that power is rarely exercised because it would call for the faculty to be of one mind on a particular issue, or at the very least to cohere in support of their head or chair. The difference between those two designators of departmental leadership, by the way, can be described quite concisely: A department head has all the power but is expected never to use it. (I remember the poignancy with which a retiring head said to me, "They all trust me now that I'm no longer going to be head.") A department chair, on the other hand, is like a gardener who is allowed to spread manure but never to weed or prune; or, as a practicing chair once said to me, "One can lead a horse to water—and watch it drown."

2. I had been dean for a few years when an old friend asked about my plans for the future: had the move up to dean exhausted my ambition or would he soon have a friend in even higher office, say, vice-president or president? "For me," I told him, "there *is* no higher office anywhere than dean of arts and sciences." Not everyone, of course, would openly agree with that, for instance, the vice-president for academic affairs. But I gathered ample proof over the years that the V-P did recognize the College of Arts and Sciences as the most important and its activities as the most interesting: a succession of V-Ps not only tried to tell me what to do with the discretionary funds supposedly at my disposal but also tried to interfere in many other ways in the college's internal affairs—far more so than in the affairs of the other colleges.

3. The functioning of universities would improve out of sight if middle-management positions were reserved for the employment of the spouses of faculty and staff and students, perhaps in some cases as half-time positions. Throughout my deanship I was saddened by the low level of competence displayed by so many of the people who held those positions, at the same time as we could not find employment for well-educated, intelligent, competent, conscientious spouses. It also infuriated me that the women's groups showed no interest in pursuing such relatively realistic possibilities nor in the gross underpayment of those women who held nonfaculty positions.

4. For example, we deans were a little bemused when our V-P once told us that all the service units reporting to his office had recently

been evaluated—the admissions office, the computing center, the library, the registrar's office. Our opinions had not been sought, nor had those of faculty, students, or chairs. Thus the efficacy of the "service" units had been judged in absence of any information about how well they served. It is also all too rarely understood that other ancillary parts of the multiversity have as their only proper function to strengthen the academic side of things, for instance, the student affairs people, the alumni groups, the student organizations, the athletics association.

5. By far most of the calls to my office were from people actually trying to reach a department or an individual member of the faculty or a student. That resulted from a decision made by the vice-president for administration that the local telephone directory should not have just one number listed for the university but separate numbers for the various colleges—the numbers of the deans' offices! In consequence, my office had to provide directory information or directory assistance for all faculty and departments in the College of Arts and Sciences. We tried to have this changed, on several occasions, to have listed just one number that would connect outside callers to the university's directory information number; but the V-P always insisted that he had not enough telephone operators to handle all that traffic. That illustrates rather well the perversely narrow view of "efficiency" that all too often prevails because there is no generally agreed and informed understanding of which functions are best centralized and which are best decentralized in the multiversity.

This tale also illustrates the running battle that pervades academic administration, each office trying to decrease the work it must do by passing some of it on to other offices. In the nature of things, the president's office can do this with the most impunity, and thus the burdens are passed down the chain of command ultimately to be assumed by the departments and the faculty. These skirmishes about who should handle what are frequently implicit only: those who are leaving or creating work for others to do are not usually prepared to acknowledge what is happening. The somewhat similar skirmishes about who should pay for what, however, are fought relatively openly. Time and again, we would find agreement quickly reached among faculty and chairs and deans and vice-president that a certain thing was worth doing—let us say, providing a computer terminal or PC for every member of the faculty and for every twenty students—but then years would pass in arguments over how much of the necessary money would come from whose budget.

A college of arts and sciences is typically at a disadvantage in arguments of that sort. Since it is usually the largest college, it usually has the largest budget of any college, and it is therefore universally presumed that it can always help out with funds that represent, after all, only a tiny fraction of its total budget. As a result, the proportion of *discretionary* funds available in the college's budget rapidly falls to zero, and it is in reality worse off than any of the other colleges. By contrast, *all* of the vice-president's budget is discretionary (as I would need to point out to him quite frequently, whenever he remarked how small were the resources available to him).

6. I suspect it will be thought that I am using my imagination rather than recounting experience when I give examples of some of the suggestions that came from our computing center and its advisors: the claim that a terminal on every desk would pay for itself through the secretarial positions that could be abolished; or the claim that even further savings would accrue when all files were maintained only in computer memory, file cabinets would be phased out, and many square feet of space would thus become available for other purposes; or that huge amounts of space could be saved by providing every member of the faculty with a terminal *at home,* thus making redundant some of the faculty offices on the campus.

For a while, indeed, every office in the central administration did have a terminal on every desk, and during my visits there I would derive surreptitious amusement from running a wet finger over the keys to gauge how long it had been since they had been touched. I also kept almost to myself my amusement at the times when the vice-presidents didn't know what they were supposed to be doing (I am speaking strictly temporally now) because their appointment calendars were kept on the computer and the computer was periodically and unpredictably "down."

At about the same time as all those terminals sprouted in the administration building, a ban was placed on the purchase of new file cabinets. After a while, the inconvenience of using large cardboard cartons for my personal files became too much for me, and I complained to my administrative assistant. "Oh, do you want another file cabinet?" she asked. "Of course," I said, "but we're not allowed to buy any." She smiled in a way that I'd seen before: "But do you really want one? Without needing to know where it came from?" And soon thereafter I had what I wanted. The V-Ps can have all the computers in Christendom, I thought, and I'm still much more fortunate than they are, because I have this assistant.

7. One of the shrewdest deans I ever met had two excellent pieces of advice for dealing with the central administration. "Always remember," he would say, "that it's much easier to get forgiveness than permission. And the way to beat them is to out-dumb them."

8. During one of my interviews for a deanship, I was asked how I would handle the nuts and bolts of administrative routine, given that there were so many nuts in the dean's office.

9. I found it remarkable that, not so long ago, the management experts discovered something called "management by objective." Then, and ever since, I've wondered what sort of management was earlier preached or practiced: management *not* by objective? Just as in the design of things to be used, form should follow function (architects and automobile manufacturers please note), so the design of organizations and procedures should follow an understanding of the functions to be performed. The function of academe is entirely different from that of industry or business or government: the less money spent by the latter, the better off the society is; but the *more* money spent on higher education, the better off the society is. And within universities, it is much better to waste a little money than to irritate the faculty.

All the vice-presidents I've known are quite intelligent and well meaning. Many of their blunders could plausibly be ascribed to their having once read a book on management per se, or to having attended a seminar on that topic, or, at any rate, to their not bearing in mind that the only proper "objective" of a college is education.

10. Barzun, for example, would not think me misguided in this: "Here and at all times, I mistrust in human affairs the ready-made design. . . . 'Policy-making' is an empty word; only daily acts give policy reality, and people do not act conformably to policy until consent and practice have bred habits. . . . the adaptation of an idea to a particular situation requires means and opportunity, like a good murder. . . ." In Jacques Barzun, *The American University—How It Runs, Where It Is Going*, New York, Evanston & London: Harper & Row, 1968; I do not give the page numbers for the quotation in the hopes that everyone will read the whole book.

11. Another and similar shibboleth would have it that "we must do so and so because everyone else does it." For example, we must recruit and admit athletes who cannot benefit from our courses, because everyone does it; we must lobby in Washington to have our projects written into laws, avoiding the traditional mode of peer review, because everyone is doing it. Where then does one draw the line? Such an attitude could also have us practice racial discrimination, say, so long as everyone else is doing it. One had piously hoped that the Nuremberg trials might have made the point that one cannot evade individual responsibility quite so easily. (For an excellent examination of that issue, see the 1961 film by Stanley Kramer, *Judgment at Nuremberg*.)

Simply going with the herd means rejecting opportunities for leadership on the implicit presumption that the voice of morality or ethics or even sense is foredoomed to impotence. That reveals a sadly low estimate of the democratic polity which, if true, would imply that a democratic republic cannot improve itself. Fortunately, there is ample empirical evidence to the contrary: say, in the improvement of workers' conditions in the last half-century, or in the elimination of legally enforced segregation over the last thirty years, or in the more recent decline in discrimination on the basis of gender.

Quite deliberate amorality is all too often practiced by academics or intellectuals who unexpectedly find themselves possessed of power: accepting the traditional view of themselves as impractical pundits and mistakenly assuming that power inevitably corrupts because it cannot be exercised ethically, they set to with an amoral vengeance and forget that the means employed determine the ends achieved. Thus, for instance, did President Kennedy's "whiz kids" recommend the ill-fated invasion of Cuba and the disastrous involvement in Vietnam.

12. Martin D. Schwartz, "An Experimental Investigation of Bad Karma and Its Relationship to the Grades of College Students: Schwartz's F.A.K.E.R. Syndrome," *Journal of Polymorphous Perversity*, 3 (1986): 9–12.

18

To Rise above Principle

Ein guter Mensch, in seinem dunklen Drange,
Ist sich den rechtes Weges wohl bewusst.[1]

—Goethe

As generalizations have exceptions, so principles should
not be followed slavishly; it has even been said that one should
beware the individual who always stands on principle. There is
also the adage that divides administrators into the two classes
of "rule-quoters" and "facilitators"; unwavering adherence to
fixed principles makes one a rule-quoter and sometime obstruc-
tionist. One wants the *spirit* behind a principle to be the guide,
not some inevitably oversimplified enunciation or formulation
of that principle. So deans must know when to make exceptions,
to principles just as to rules. But of course they must not be
capricious: they should disregard principles only in a principled, not in an unprincipled, manner.

For example, a few years ago some federal legislators began
to treat certain large university projects as just so much (or more)
pork barrel: instead of leaving it to the National Science Foundation, say, to determine which university was best equipped
to set up, say, a supercomputer, bills were written not to fund
a supercomputer but a supercomputer *at a particular place.*

Strong protests came from the academic community against this rejection of perceived ability or merit as the determining criterion in the awarding of research funds; and such protests came even from places that might have received some of the pork barrel. One bill would have assigned a supercomputer to Cornell University, but the president of that university publicly criticized the bill, disclaimed any part in the maneuver, and said that Cornell would not accept a supercomputer under those circumstances. I was profoundly distressed when one of our vice-presidents commented that Cornell's president would not get much support in this from his faculty: "Such grandstanding," said the V-P, "is a fine example of letting principles get in the way of getting things done."

But surely that is precisely a proper function of principles: they *should* prevent us from doing certain sorts of things. Only by recognizing *categories* of behavior, and labeling some of them inappropriate or unworthy or unethical or immoral, can we be ready in any particular situation to act ethically rather than simply from desire. One knows, of course, that it is not always possible to fit all possible human actions into a number of discrete categories—there will be some doubtful or marginal cases; and it is then that we must be ready to make exceptions to our principles. However, as I hope the following will illustrate, such exceptions might best be described as *apparent* exceptions to the relevant principle, certainly not as *disregarding* the principle, which that V-P would have had Cornell's president do.

*   *   *   *   *

Honesty, it is said, is the best policy, and I agree wholeheartedly—as, for instance, when John Doe was waving his offer from Someplace Else alternately in his chair's face and in mine. We don't match offers, I told him; they are always above market value, and so on (see chapter 13). Sometime later, Doe's chair shared his amusement with me: "I was telling Doe that we don't match offers, and that the salaries offered are always inflated because a move costs a lot in all ways, and all the rest. And when I was through, he looked at me in amazement and said, 'But

that's just what the dean told me!' Isn't it marvelous? All one
has to do is to tell the truth, and life becomes awfully simple."

Because, for instance, if one habitually tells lies, one had better have an extraordinarily good memory, to recall which lie
was told to whom. . . . But, of course, as that chair knew as well
as I, we *had* sometimes bargained with one who had an offer in
hand. Weren't we both really lying to Doe?

I would always point out that salary adjustments could only
be made at one time in each year: recommendations in the spring,
approval by the Governing Board in the summer, new salary to
take effect at the beginning of the next academic year. Nothing
else was possible, I would say. But, of course, in a couple of
cases we *did* raise salaries in mid-year.

"I never negotiate with a member of the faculty about salary,
teaching load, or anything else," I had occasion to say not infrequently; "that is between you and your chair." But on at least
one occasion I did: without consulting the chair first, I guaranteed a lighter teaching load for an exceptional individual.

"The university has no mechanism for making positions available to spouses, be it of people being hired or of people already
on the faculty," I had occasion to say more and more frequently.
But, of course, there were occasions when various strings were
pulled and spouses were hired whom we would not have hired
from the open market.

"We have no funds to support the publishing of journals";
but we did sometimes find them. "We never approve a third
successive year of leave without pay"; but we did, a few times.
"Sabbaticals cannot be granted before six full years of service
have elapsed"; but we found a way around that when it seemed
desirable.

Was I lying when I said "never," knowing full well that the
truth was "rarely"? I don't think so. Paul Halmos has put it very
nicely: "There is a difference between misleading statements
and false ones; striving for 'the clear reception of the message'
you are sometimes allowed to lie a little, but you must never
mislead. . . . A part of the art of lecturing is to know when and

how to lie. Don't insist on protecting yourself by being cowardly legalistic, but lead the audience to the truth."[2]

And so with administrators as with teachers. If the dean tells a professor or a chair that an exception is possible, what is heard is that *you may be prepared to make an exception in this case,* not that an exception is possible in principle, though only very rarely and almost certainly not in this case.

One of my friends once worked for a V-P who didn't understand that. Faculty and chairs would come away from meetings with him aglow with optimism, for he never said "No." Anything was possible; they should explore it with the dean. . . .

"But," my friend the dean would then have to explain to his visitors, "we can't just offer a named chair like that. When one of those is vacant, the V-P issues a call for nominations. Then the departments nominate, and the College Committee ranks, and the University Committee advises, and the V-P chooses. Now admittedly in the past the university sometimes used these positions to hire exceptional people from elsewhere, but just in the last year we had from the V-P the memo I passed on to you at the time, that for the foreseeable future these titles would only be awarded after open competition among current faculty."

"But we've just been to the V-P," would come the response, "and he assured us that it was possible."

So the dean would have to forward the department's request formally to the V-P. When it was then rejected, of course the department blamed my friend the dean for not making the case properly or strongly enough, whereas they should have blamed the V-P for misleading them. In Halmos's terms, the V-P was being cowardly legalistic and telling the literal truth: it was possible, as he said; but since he had not intended it to happen in this instance, he had misled, and thereby sinned more egregiously than if he had merely lied a little.

*　　*　　*　　*　　*

There is an overriding reason for not admitting that exceptions are possible: with a little ingenuity—which students and faculty possess no less than do other self-interested human beings—anyone can evolve reasons why an exception should be made in any given case, reasons moreover that are not entirely implausible or invalid. Why not give a third year of leave without pay, for example? After all, the university saves either the whole salary or that part of it not needed for the much cheaper temporary replacement. And if it is good for the university to have its faculty being visible around the country, how better than by having them also in a regular position elsewhere?[3] All that new and varied experience will be brought back to our campus once the leave is at last over. And so on.

Entering into that sort of discussion, let us be clear, amounts to opening up the whole question for which a policy already exists. Presumably these general pros and cons were considered when the university, through its regular and thorough procedures of governance, came to adopt the policy that two years would be the maximum length of time for which leaves without pay would be granted. Therefore no arguments *of a general nature* can be valid arguments for an exception to policy: valid exceptions, exceptions that a dean can properly seek to bring about, must have to do with idiosyncratic particularities of the case at hand, particularities that would make the exception fit better the *spirit* of the policy, or particularities that point to some overriding interest of the university. Therefore I recommended an exceptional third year of leave, for example, only in two extreme sorts of cases: for people we desperately wanted to keep or to entice back and who could not bring themselves to forsake a professional opportunity temporarily available elsewhere; or, more commonly, for people we desperately didn't want back on campus and who would have returned rather than resigned if we had not granted the extra leave.

Rather obviously, those are not reasons to which one could admit in public; nor are they reasons that one can usefully share with an individual who is requesting an exception. It is better to tell someone for whom an exception is not going to be made, "We never make such exceptions," than "We do this for some people, but we will not do it for you." It is gratuitous to remind those who are good but not outstanding that they are good but not outstanding; their career of salary raises and time between promotions has given the message clearly enough, and they are serving the university conscientiously and to the best of their ability, and they can only serve better if they feel appreciated and worse if they feel denigrated.

Thus honesty may not always be the best policy—though I personally would maintain that it is, just so long as one defines honesty in Halmosian terms. No matter what conclusion a dean arrives at on this issue, however, he must be clear and honest with himself about it. If not, then he will sometimes feel like a hypocrite; and one who feels like a hypocrite *is* a hypocrite, by definition; and people tend to recognize a hypocrite when they encounter one. Now a dean should lead, should enunciate and promulgate ideals and principles, and he cannot do that convincingly while feeling hypocritical. So a dean must be able to hold the highest ideals about means as well as about ends, and to work toward them, all the while knowing that he will sometimes fall short, and not necessarily by his own fault. I've heard no better expression of what the ideals ought to be than from my friend Paul, when he was exercised at a news report that some eminent personage whose hobby was golf—perhaps it was President Eisenhower?—had confessed the ambition to break 80.

"Good God," groaned Paul in disgust, "what sort of an ambition is that? If *I* were a golfer, I wouldn't be trying to break 80; I'd be trying to break 18!"

I used that line when I was asked during an interview how I should like to be remembered after my term as dean was over. I would want to be remembered, I answered, as having been fair and trustworthy, and that represented a practical minimum that I felt I could achieve. But in truth I would be trying, in my friend's terms, to break 18.

*　　*　　*　　*　　*

There is at least one principle that should be held inviolate: the dean must practice personal loyalty—to the staff, to the department chairs, to the V-P, and to the president. The dean may not, for instance, confidentially and in candor speak ill of a chair or of the V-P to a member of the faculty. That is not to say that a dean cannot express reservations about particular policies and even hopes or intentions to seek changes; but a dean must never leave a professor in any doubt that the dean supports the chair and thinks he should be chair; and that the dean supports the V-P and thinks he should be V-P. So, with a few faculty who, I thought, the university badly needed to keep and to keep happy, I would permit myself some such comments as these, about a chair, say: "I have to agree that he is not perfect; but then I don't know anyone who is. Remember how he built this program, and how good he was when that student made that unjustified complaint. You can't always have such strength *and* the ultimate in sensitive finesse. I'm sure he didn't intend to be abrupt with you," and so on.

I could agree, in other words, with expressed criticism of a chair only to the extent of putting it into perspective, indicating that I was not blind to blemishes but was firmly of the mind that, overall, the chair was our best option. Professors being human, and humans being apt to hear selectively, it is not possible for a dean to admit to a professor that he disagrees with a chair and yet leave a convincing and lasting impression that the chair nevertheless has the dean's full support. It is of overriding importance that the dean's full support for the chairs and for the staff be universally known.

*   *   *   *   *

I've often recalled my first day on the job. My assistant brought me a foot-high stack of things to sign, including papers of appointment for a number of people and other nontrivial matters. Now I believe strongly in paying attention to detail, but I realized then and there that life would be insupportable if I could not trust my assistant. So I asked her to explain in quick outline what the various papers were, and I signed them forthwith. And that may have been the best decision I ever made as dean.

Looking back, I think that she may have been testing me—would I or would I not give her my trust? And as I passed the test, I came to benefit from the highest degree of loyalty from her.

Trust in a relationship is entirely mutual. If you show that you trust your staff, then they will trust you. But if you allow it to be seen that you do not trust your staff, then they will *know* that they cannot trust you. If you are always liable to second-guess them, or if they can never know whether or not you will back them, then they can't do their jobs properly, and they certainly can't get any satisfaction from doing them, and they can't trust you or feel any loyalty toward you.

Part of the necessary trust is to let people do things in their own way—if only because there is no other way that anyone can do anything. Your staff will quickly learn the important things about what you want: whether the office is to be facilitating or bureaucratic, stiffly formal or scrupulously informal or somewhere in-between; whether you are more concerned with principles or with regulations; and they will take their lead from you without elaborate explicit instruction. In turn, you must respect their way of doing things—and bite your tongue at things that might offend your sense of style a bit but that don't really matter all that much, certainly nothing like as much as the trust and devotion of your staff.

Occasionally the criticism would reach my ears, that I tended to be too loyal to my staff and to the department chairs. In all honesty, I would cheerfully accept that as my epitaph.[4]

*   *   *   *   *

The dean's loyalty has to be directed upward as well as sideways and down; the dean's full support of the vice-president and the president must be common knowledge. The administrative chain of command through which existing policy is implemented (by contrast to the committee structure of governance through which policy is made) has no room for a publicly vocal "loyal opposition" (see note 1 to chapter 12). In private, of course, the dean must press his contrary views on the vice-president; and inevitably a dean of arts and sciences arrives at different views than does a vice-president or a president. The latter must find accommodations between the intellectual role of the university and many other things: legislatures and governors, alumni and athletics; in the case of the professional colleges, the pressures brought by accrediting agencies, farm bureaus, societies of professional engineers, and the like. All too few of the matters that come to the dean are black or white; even less so for the V-P, let alone the P.

No vice-president and no president, I recognized, could always act according to my liking. Thus the V-P ought, in my view, to starve some of the other colleges, and some of the "service" operations, and give this college more of what we so badly needed. But it is his proper job *not* to do that: he is supposed to seek excellence not only in the arts and sciences but also in agriculture and engineering and medicine, and through the colleges of communications and of education and of home economics and the rest (difficult as it might be for me to imagine what excellence in some of those areas could mean). Thus the V-P and the dean *must* differ over some matters; but they can work together productively and even amicably if they recognize and respect the different responsibilities that they bear;[5] and so too between the president and the dean.

*   *   *   *   *

In private arguments with the vice-president or the president, a dean of arts and sciences has the luxury of having an impeccable case to push. Within the university, that college is unique, in part because it serves three distinct and worthy functions whereas the other colleges have only the single one of preparing their students for a particular profession. Arts and sciences also prepares students for particular professions, of course (albeit largely at the graduate rather than the undergraduate level), but in addition it provides much of the fundamental instruction for students of the other colleges, prerequisites for the specialized and applied work in engineering and agriculture and the rest; and, most important, the college of arts and sciences provides whatever general and liberal education the university happens to offer or require. And education of that sort matters; it matters very much indeed. In fact it matters more than any other sort: as Jacques Barzun has put it, instruction is necessary because we are not born human, though we may learn to become so.

Biologically, humans are not all that special. A human who knows only biologically, instinctively, emotionally, is just another mammal—a marvelous enough thing in itself, of course, but not what we most prize about humanity. It is culturally that human beings are very special indeed. And so to become human means to become cultured: it means to learn about humanity's history and its literature and its religion, about its sciences and technologies and arts; it means to become aware of what the best minds have thought about human existence. And the study of those things is the business of arts and sciences. We are the ones for whom it is a vocation, and we are the ones who can do it best, for we are the ones who extend the boundaries of understanding in the disciplines that deal in the purest form with knowledge and with understanding.

Ours is a secular society, not a religious one: religion gave way to science when the latter proved to give more believable answers about the world around us. But in discarding religious dogma we also lost the basis for our ethical codes. We insist now that moral and ethical teachings be understandable in human terms and that they be consonant with science, yet no satisfactory system along those lines has emerged, and so we are proselytized by many competing sects, secular as well as religious: secular humanists and fundamentalists, sociobiologists and Christian Scientists, Marxists and spiritualists. Amid this welter, the best preparation we can give our children is to teach them as much as possible of what we have learned about humanity and about nature and to make them aware of the seductions of dogma, of the wishfulness that can cause us to accept some beliefs against our better judgment. We must bring our children as far as possible to think analytically and critically.

And that, of course, is what a liberal education is all about. No other college and nothing else in society has this as its professional preoccupation, as its inescapable responsibility. We stand for learning—learning for its own sake—and we insist that nothing else is so relevant. "Relevant to what?" we used to be asked. "Relevant to all aspects of human life," is the answer we should have given.

But what about ethics, morals, values? What does learning history or mathematics or chemistry have to do with that?

That question is based on the erroneous premise that what we are doing is solely the transmitting of some knowledge. But if we do the transmitting well, then it is not at all "solely," for we are also helping our students to learn how to learn. We give them practice in scrutinizing texts and statements, in deciding what to accept and what to reject and what to leave neither rejected nor accepted for the time being.

Learning how to learn, and learning how to learn for its own sake, instills some important values. It instills honesty, because there is no such thing as dishonest learning. Individual students and individual teachers may of course practice dishonesty, but only to the extent that they don't care about learning—their own learning or that of others; thus students who cheat on examinations are only cheating themselves. Learning is a hard taskmaster; in fact, there is no way to "beat the system": you learn honestly or you don't learn at all.

Learning offers ample opportunity to acquire a decent humility. Those who attempt to learn honestly can hardly fail to acknowledge their own limitations. We wrestle long and hard to understand, and then, having achieved some understanding, we realize how simple and obvious it all is, how easy to grasp— except that it was difficult for us and was achieved perhaps more readily by doubtless many others besides and before us. And as we progress, our increased understanding of some things makes all the sharper and clearer, by contrast, our total lack of understanding of so many other things. True scholars, in their hearts and in their own fields, are driven to humility.

Further, one can hardly love and practice learning without acquiring some respect for the differing opinions of others, because honest learning so often demands that we change from our earlier views; it shows us that others can be right about matters on which we have been wrong. In learning about humanity's cultural progress, we learn that the greatest of minds have differed over important matters and continue to do so.

But chiefly, the commitment to learning for its own sake, to scholarship and the search for truth, is in itself a very strong statement of values held and advocated. It is, moreover, a statement of values entirely consistent with the values of this republic and its Constitution. It advocates the best and greatest learning for every individual; it advocates education rather than indoctrination; it manifests the faith that free and well-educated people will not succumb to authoritarian or totalitarian dogmas.

Notes

1. The quote is from *Faust*, I:328–29. I have not found a published translation that seems just right. Perhaps the closest is by Walter Kaufmann (Garden City, N.Y.: Doubleday, 1961; Anchor Books, 1963):
    A good man in his darkling aspiration
    Remembers the right road throughout his quest.
Translating in isolation from the body of the text, unconcerned about rhyme or meter, one might put it like this:
    Through all the darkling struggles of life,
    a good man still knows well enough, what the right way is.
2. Paul R. Halmos, *I Want to Be a Mathematician*, New York, Berlin, Heidelberg & Tokyo: Springer-Verlag, 1985, pp. 113–14. The whole book makes rewarding reading.
3. I said "regular position" here because we occasionally had requests for leaves without pay to permit someone tenured in our university to try out a position elsewhere for a year or two before committing unequivocally to it. That seemed to me unethical from the standpoint of that other institution, apart from anything else; on the other hand, should one refuse a person who put this openly to us, and

yet permit others to do it who lied to us, representing their tryout period as a purely visiting arrangement?

I recall an occasion when a professor, whom we had hired as a visitor while he was on sabbatical leave from his home university, came to sound me out. Our department, he said, had indicated that they would like him to join them permanently. How did I view that? Why, I would listen to the chair, of course. If the department had a vacant position, and if I could be shown that there was reason to leave it in that department, and to appoint someone at a senior rank and in that subspecialty. . . . That was just normal routine. Of course, matters between him and his present university were solely for him to negotiate. We had a policy whereby people who took sabbatical leaves were obliged to return to us for two full years after the leave or to reimburse the university for the appropriate part of the salary paid during the leave. Did his university have a similar policy? Did they enforce it always or could it be waived?

As it turned out, our department did subsequently make the case, and Professor Mayhew of Elsewhere College became a full professor with tenure in our university.

Halfway through the next academic year, the mail delivered the following to my desk:

Dear Dean Martin:

As you know, Professor Mayhew joined your faculty immediately after enjoying a sabbatical leave from this college. Our regulations state that in such a case we are to be reimbursed for the salary paid during the leave; and it seemed appropriate to request your university rather than the individual to do so. In fact, that is what we have done in similar circumstances.

Consequently, we would appreciate receiving at your convenience the sum of $27,700:

Salary at half pay	$20,000
Fringe benefits	
@ 30%	6,000
FICA	1,200
Travel grant for leave	500
TOTAL	$27,700

Yours sincerely,
I. M. Hopeful
Dean of the Faculty

Some sort of a reply seemed to be necessary.

> Dear Dean Hopeful:
>
> I was a little surprised by your letter, having advised Professor Mayhew at the time of the negotiations that he would need to settle the matter of the leave stipulations directly with you. In any case, this university has no mechanism for making the sort of payment that you request.
>
> Perhaps, however, I could put to our administration the desirability of instituting such a policy, supporting that suggestion with the argument that other institutions do this (though I had not previously been aware of any that do). Could you perhaps give me specific details of the instances you mentioned in which Elsewhere College has made such payments?
>
> Most sincerely,
J. Martin
>
> cc:V-P, Academic Affairs
>   Professor Mayhew

I was never able to take the matter further because I received no reply. Nor had I expected one, of course. The purpose of Hopeful's letter, I had assumed, was to make sure that we were aware that Mayhew had behaved unethically toward his previous college. That I sent Mayhew a copy of my reply was doubtless a sufficient indication to Hopeful that his message had been received, understood, and passed on.

4. Perhaps because I know how similarly necessary it was for me to have the V-P's trust. Happy was the dean who could roast the president in these terms: "He is too up-beat all the time, which drives me up the wall; he is far too loyal to the people who work with him; and he is too kind. And it occurs to me that with those vices, perhaps he doesn't need any virtues. . . ."

5. Similarly, faculty and chairs must recognize that it is the dean's job to support all the fields within the college, even while they believe that their own subspecialty and department are the most worthy and the most needy. Some individuals can't manage that, of course; for instance, Professor Petty, the first-rate scientist who protested that I had supported the establishment of a unit for interdisciplinary studies in the humanities and the social sciences. How could I put resources

into that, he wanted to know, "when it isn't even hard science?" Since
that occasion I've wondered several times how—or even whether—
Petty had thought about the matter. Could he seriously believe that
a dean of arts and sciences ought to support only the hard sciences?
Quite possibly, I usually concluded. Common sense and practicality
are surely at a premium for deans, but those qualities are rarely needed
in the higher realms of scholarship or research.

A Note on the Author

Josef Martin had attained a respectable reputation in his scholarly field, with a publication list stretching toward the three-figure mark, before he took up deaning. He has held appointments at half-a-dozen places and in four countries, deploying his administrative talents in behalf of research programs and professional societies as well as deaning. He has published and lectured on popular as well as scholarly subjects. This is his sixth book.